CHARACTER

OLD TESTAMENT PEOPLE—
ENCOUNTERS WITH GOD

BY RICHARD PARKER

youth
specialties

Character: Old Testament People—Encounters with God
Copyright 2008 Clarity Publishers, Inc.

Youth Specialties resources, 300 S. Pierce St., El Cajon, CA 92020 are published by Zondervan, 5300 Patterson Ave. SE, Grand Rapids, MI 49530.

ISBN 978-0-310-27906-8

Published in association with Yates & Yates, LLP, Attorneys and Counselors, Orange, California

Cover design by Brandi K. Etheredge
Interior design by SharpSeven Design

Printed in the United States of America

08 09 10 11 12 • 20 19 18 17 16 15 14 13 12 11 10 9 8 7 6 5 4 3 2 1

CONTENTS

INTRO

HOW TO USE THIS BOOK

The people of the Old Testament were flawed. In this journal you'll find stories of broken family relationships, deceit, adultery, and compromise. However, the Old Testament isn't really about the people. It's about a God who loves his creation. In this 48-week journal, you'll see how God has led people of every generation to respond to him in faith and obedience. The features of this journal will help you dig into the Bible. Here's how to get the most from your time with God:

Introduction: These are short sections that introduce each week of devotionals. If you're studying the CHARACTER series on Sunday mornings, Wednesday nights, or in small groups, then each week of devotions will coincide with what you're studying in class. Read the Introduction section to get a picture of what the week's devotions will center on.

Daily Devotions: Now we're getting to the good stuff. This journal is designed to walk you through five days of devotions each week. And each devotion contains a Scripture passage and a paragraph of text. Always start by reading the Scripture passage in your Bible, and then read the text. Look for ways that the text unlocks some truths of Scripture you may not have noticed before.

Daily Questions: After each devotional paragraph, you'll find questions designed to get you thinking. When you read these questions, take a moment to really consider what they're asking. Listen to the Holy Spirit as he teaches you through Scripture. Then record your thoughts in the Journal Space.

Journal Spaces: You'll notice this book is different from many books you've read because it's designed to be filled with your thoughts. Use the space provided to record your reactions to each devotional passage. Or use it to write a prayer request or praise to God. Use it any way you please. It's your journal. There are no rules, just guidelines. The important thing is to listen to God and open your heart in response to his leading.

If you take the time to read the devotionals prayerfully and with the anticipation God will reveal new things to you, then you'll be amazed at what will flow through your pen or pencil and onto the pages.

GOD'S CHARACTER AND OURS

When you think of the words Old Testament, what's the first thing that comes to mind?

Maybe other words—such as Moses, Genesis, history book, old men with long beards, or Ten Commandments. That's not exactly page-turning excitement at first glance. While all these words might work for a particular spot of the Old Testament, let's look at the big picture. Think about the word testament.

Today we might think of a testament as a testimony—as evidence of something. And the Old Testament is a kind of testimony. It's evidence of God's movement through history. But the way testament was first used meant covenant. So what's a covenant? It's the relationship God made with his people. If you're a believer in Jesus Christ, then you're in a covenant with God. From the time he created the world, God has been reaching out to people—characters—in order to have relationships with them.

When Jesus came, he created a new relationship between God and people. (That's why the Old Testament is old and the New Testament is new.) As a Christian, you're part of the new relationship. But to understand the relationship you have with God, you need to know where you came from. You need to know the past to understand your present and future. We'll never fully understand the message of the

New Testament if we don't know the Old. We'll miss so much in the Christian life if we don't understand the Old Testament.

The pages of the Old Testament are filled with stories about people. We'll call them "characters." Sometimes it's hard to understand they were real people just like us. They had issues and problems. Some led righteous lives. Others failed to follow God's ways. Just as we do, they had their struggles and triumphs. This 48-week journal covers the same issues and problems we still talk about thousands of years later. We long for a perfect creation, fulfilled promises, and deliverance from slavery. We talk about things such as haircuts, dreams, feasts, and love. We gaze with suspense at spies, war, adultery, betrayal, and famine. And we dream about royalty, prophecy, visions, and beauty—just like the Old Testament characters. Times may change, but people stay pretty much the same.

God didn't include these characters in the Bible just so we could read a good story. He included them to reveal himself—his character—to us. That makes this more than a study on Old Testament characters. This series is about God. After all, he's the One who created each character. He's the One who brought them into relationship with himself, gave them purpose, and used them for his glory. And just as he worked in the lives of those characters, he desires to work in yours. Let's get started.

WEEK 1
JESUS AND THE OLD TESTAMENT

MEMORY VERSE

"Do not think that I have come to abolish the Law or the Prophets; I have not come to abolish them but to fulfill them." (Matthew 5:17)

INTRODUCTION

Welcome to a yearlong journey through the Old Testament! *Boring* is the word some might use when the Old Testament is mentioned, but over the next 48 weeks you'll discover that the first part of the Bible is anything but boring. If you like mystery, intrigue, suspense, heroes, villains, and the kind of action that would put many video games to shame, then you're going to love the Old Testament.

Each week you'll discover how a character in the Old Testament was affected by faith in God. Right now, list your five favorite Old Testament characters.

1.

2.

3.

4.

5.

Did you include Jesus in your list? Jesus? Yes, Jesus! He's the main character of the Old Testament because in Jesus we find the true meaning of the Scriptures.

In the life of each Old Testament character, God was preparing his people to find redemption in Jesus Christ. When you put your faith in God through Jesus, you're actually fulfilling the purpose of the Bible.

Sometimes we focus on the miracles God did in the Old Testament, but remember that each event was performed for one reason: To point people to a God who loved them. In every over-the-top, blow-your-mind movement, God had the same simple message and the same simple purpose: To let humanity experience his awesome love.

Hint: One way to remember the books of the Old Testament is to remember two numbers—5 and 12. The 39 books are grouped into five subcategories: Five books of law, five books of poetry, five major prophets, a dozen books of history, and another dozen minor prophets.

DAILY DEVOTIONS

Day 1
Matthew 5:17-20

Today's passage comes from a message Jesus preached to his followers. It's been called the Sermon on the Mount. Many scholars have referred to this passage as Jesus' greatest teaching.

The Jews believed strict obedience to the Old Testament Law was the way to be right with God. So Jesus' teachings angered the Jewish leaders. Jesus explained that he is the fulfillment of the Law; he's the reason the Law was written.

Imagine you take out a $10,000 bank loan. You aren't making much money, so each month you pay only the interest on the loan. How long do you believe it will take you to pay off the loan? If you're financially sharp, then you may have already realized that you'll never pay off the debt if all you pay is the interest.

In a similar way, the Jewish leaders had set up a system of Law-keeping in order to have a relationship with God. They thought they could pay off their sin debt by sacrificing animals and following the Jewish Law. It was like paying interest only—the real debt was never fully paid. But when Jesus said he was the fulfillment of the Law, he was saying he'd come to pay off the complete debt of sin. Christ has paid your entire debt.

Write a prayer to God and thank him for sending Jesus to pay your sin debt.

Day 2
Luke 24:25-27

There was a television show that aired in the 1950s called *What's My Line*? The game show involved four panelists who took turns asking a mystery guest questions in order to determine his identity. At the end of the show, the mystery guest revealed his identity.

After his resurrection, Jesus appeared to some of his believers on the road to Emmaus. Jesus told them the Old Testament pointed to a mystery guest—a Savior who'd one day come and save God's people. The believers had no idea they were talking to the risen Christ. Later, their "blindfolds" were removed, and they realized they were talking to Jesus.

Jesus has been at work in your life and trying to communicate with you this week. Have you seen him?

As you think back over the past few days, what's happened that was probably God working in your life?

Day 3
John 5:37-43

Some people can talk big, but they rarely back up their claims. You may know some people like that. "Too much talk and not enough action" is what we usually say about those people.

The Jewish leaders were upset that Jesus not only broke Sabbath laws but also claimed he was equal to God. They accused Jesus of being a "big claim" kind of guy. But Jesus could back up his claims. He was the Son of God. Whenever you read your Bible, keep an eye out for some of the big claims Jesus made, and remember this one thing: He came through each time and never made a claim he didn't fulfill.

Day 4
John 8:34-43

A man once escaped from prison by digging his way out through a tunnel and breaking through the floor of a preschool daycare facility.

The prisoner shouted, "I'm free! I'm free!" to which a preschooler replied, "Well, I'm four."

The Jews understood Jesus' words on freedom about as well as the preschooler understood the prisoner's. The Jews thought they were free because of their relationship to Abraham. But Jesus said only the Son can set you free. And once he sets you free, you're totally free!

Day 5
Romans 10:1-4

Every good story has a beginning, a middle, and an end. In the beginning you see the problem. In the middle you see how the problem is going to be resolved. And in the end you understand what life is like after the resolution. But to get the whole story, you have to read more than the last chapter of the book. Just like if you walk into a movie and see only the last 30 minutes, then you're likely to be lost.

The story of God is the same way—it's found throughout the whole Bible, but it begins in the Old Testament where the problem of sin is introduced, and it just gets worse. However, with the arrival of Jesus in the New Testament, the solution to the problem becomes clear: Jesus is the only possible solution. Then after the story of Jesus, the early church is birthed and everything is changed by the work of Christ.

Have you ever read the Bible from cover to cover? As we begin this journey, why not commit to reading the entire Old Testament this year? Some parts of the Old Testament are hard reading, but when you understand this part of God's revelation, his truth will come alive in ways you haven't experienced before.

WEEK 2
GOD, THE PERFECT CREATOR

MEMORY VERSE

"So God created man in his own image, in the image of God he created him; male and female he created them." (Genesis 1:27)

INTRODUCTION

When I was in the eighth grade, I had a science teacher who loved to teach about evolution and the Big Bang Theory. Evolution is a theory that all life forms have evolved from lower life forms. The Big Bang Theory says an explosion of molecules created the universe. Neither of these theories leaves much room for a heavenly Father who created this world. So one day in class I asked my teacher about her theory, and she kept going back in time until she reached a point where a single cell collided with other single cells and creation started.

"But where did that single cell come from?" I asked. The teacher said I just had to have faith that single cells have always existed. "That's the difference between you and me," I said. "You put your faith in a single cell, and I put my faith in God the Creator."

The Bible begins with the story of creation. God created an orderly world in an orderly fashion. Each phase of the creation process was done with planning and purpose, and the end result was and is spectacular. While a beautiful sunset and a cascading waterfall are beautiful, God's pride and joy—out of all the things he created—is you. He created you, and he gave you this beautiful world to live in.

How should we respond? Two ways we can respond to God's marvelous work of creation are to thank him and to take care of the world around us.

DAILY DEVOTIONS

Day 1
Genesis 1:1-2

If you could get an immediate answer, what one question would you ask God?

I tossed out that possibility to my students one Wednesday night, and here are some of their questions for God:

> *"How did you come about?"*
> *"Where did you come from?"*
> *"How can you have no beginning and no end?"*
> *"Are there really aliens stored in Area 51?"*

The Bible opens with the simple statement, "In the beginning God..." If you ever get discouraged because you don't know the answers to all your questions, be encouraged by that statement—because in the end, that's all we have to know. God has always been and always will be. Accepting that truth is just a matter of faith. One day God will answer all our questions—even the ones about Area 51. For now, accept by faith the claims of God. That's all you need to do; that's all you need to believe.

As you pray this week, remember that God never minds getting questions from honest seekers.

Day 2
Genesis 1:3-5

To appreciate light, one must experience the dark. The darkest experience I've ever had was in Mammoth Cave in Kentucky. When the tour guide turned off the lights in the cave, I actually felt the cold emptiness of the pitch blackness. I held my hand up to my face, and I couldn't even see a hint of my fingers. That's how dark the world was until God spoke and created the light.

The world is still in darkness, although the darkness we experience today is spiritual. People cannot see what's true—that God loves them and wants a relationship with them—even though that truth is right in front of their faces. God is calling you to be a light in the world. Will you answer that challenge?

Why do people choose to live in spiritual darkness when God's light is available to them?

What are some ways you can be a spiritual light in your world today?

Day 3
Genesis 1:11-13

Sometimes the little things in this world are really amazing. When God created plants, he made each one to produce seeds of its own kind so his creation would continue to grow. Look around your world today. Every living thing grew from a seed from something God created. He created everything to reproduce—even people. What about spiritual reproduction?

What about your life would demonstrate to people you come in contact with today that you're a Christian?

Write the names of three people you'll see today who, as far as you know, aren't Christians. Make a commitment to pray for those people each day this week.

Day 4
Genesis 1:26

Oakland, California, has a massive interstate highway system. State workers maintain the roads and pick up litter. But, as you can imagine, keeping those roads clean is a huge task. Along a one-mile stretch of interstate leading into the city, workers pick up an average of seven large trash bags of debris every day.

God created humans and gave them rule over the earth. Part of that responsibility includes taking care of this world. If one of your friends came to visit you and left your home a wreck, your parents would probably tell you not to invite him back. A good guest always leaves things as they were—if not better.

As Christians, we're simply guests on this planet because it isn't our permanent home. We can show our appreciation to God for his creation by taking good care of it.

Day 5
Genesis 2:1-3

God rested. Can you believe it? The supreme Creator of the entire universe took time to rest. It makes me think that if God took time to rest, then we probably need to do the same. Many people say God really didn't need to rest. He is God, after all. Resting, some may say, was just a way to show us the importance of taking a break from our hectic schedules in order to spend some time with God. But think about it...maybe rest isn't just a good idea. Maybe rest is an actual necessity.

Sometimes a circus will have a plate spinner. He puts a plate on the top of a stick and starts spinning it. Then he puts another plate on another stick and starts spinning it as well. Good plate spinners can have 10 or 12 plates spinning at once. The problem is if a plate quits spinning, it crashes to the ground. So the plate spinner runs from plate to plate, spinning them a bit faster to keep them balanced.

You may have lots of plates spinning as well. You run from one event to the next, desperately trying to keep your commitments from crashing to the ground. Think about the time you invest each week in school, sports, family, church, and so on. God didn't create us to live in the fast lane. He said, "Be still, and know that I am God" (Psalm 46:10).

WEEK 3
ADAM AND EVE'S DEADLY DECISION

MEMORY VERSE

"The God of peace will soon crush Satan under your feet. The grace of our Lord Jesus be with you." (Romans 16:20)

INTRODUCTION

Celebrities and sports stars seem to have it all. They have fame; they have incredible abilities; they're often good-looking; and they have lots and lots of money. Then you read about a big-name personality who destroys his life. He loses it all because of an addiction, bad choices, or just boredom with the celebrity lifestyle. How can a person who has it all make such bad decisions?

The first two people in the Bible had it all. Adam and Eve had a great life with the opportunity to talk personally with God every day. But then they blew it with one bad decision. It doesn't seem fair to lose so much so quickly based on just one mistake, but that's exactly what happened.

Adam and Eve's story is really the story of every person who's ever walked on this earth. We all experience the temptation to disregard God's will and do what we want. The temptation to disobey God—to sin—leads to physical and spiritual consequences. If nothing is done about our sin, then it will lead us to death and hell.

The good news is there's a way out. We can choose to turn from sin and accept God's forgiveness. Adam and Eve chose to seek forgiveness, and God did forgive them—but the consequences were huge. Their wonderful lives came to an abrupt end, and they had to live with the negative consequences of that one bad decision for the rest of their lives.

DAILY DEVOTIONS

Day 1
Genesis 2:4-15

I like going places I've never been and seeing things I've never seen. I visited Niagara Falls for the first time in 1991, and I'll never forget the sense of awe and wonder I felt as I stood so close to one of the wonders of the world. Do you remember the first time you saw a mountain or an ocean? Do you remember that sense of "Wow!"?

Since he was the first person God created, Adam was the first to see the wonder and beauty of God's creation. He was the first person to see a sunrise or a sunset. Adam had a lifetime of firsts in just one day. Needless to say, he was probably pretty wiped out just from saying, "Wow!"

God has a "wow" experience waiting for you today. Don't miss it!

Day 2
Genesis 2:15-25

One of the classic case studies in the field of psychology involved two groups of children placed on two different playgrounds of the same size, one with fences and one without fences. The children who played in the unfenced area all tended to play close to each other and right in the middle of the playground. The children in the fenced area played all over the place, especially right along the fence. The fence actually created a greater sense of freedom for the children.

Many people see the Bible as just a big book of do's and don'ts. They don't realize God places limits—fences—in our lives to protect us. So the fences, which may be seen as negatives, are actually positives.

Thank God for the protection—and the freedom—he provides for us through his Word.

Day 3
Ephesians 6:1-3

A fence has two purposes: It can keep something in, or it can keep something out. Your parents have probably tried to put up some fences in your life. You may believe those fences are to keep you in—to keep you caged so you can't have any fun. In fact, your parents have probably tried to put fences in place to protect you by keeping some things out of your life. That's certainly a different way of looking at it.

The Bible is very clear about our response to those fences: "Children, obey your parents in the Lord, for this is right" (Ephesians 6:1).

Day 4
Genesis 3:8-13

Have you noticed that in our society not many people take responsibility for anything?

A woman sued a fast-food chain because she burned herself by spilling a cup of their hot coffee. She claimed she wasn't adequately warned that the coffee was hot. Call me naive, but if I order a cup of coffee and it's not hot, then there's a problem. I know a high school teacher who got a call from a 34-year-old former student who said her life was ruined because the teacher didn't properly encourage her.

Don't get me wrong. Warning labels on coffee cups are fine, and I agree that teachers should try to encourage their students. Still, I believe we'd all be a lot better off if we accepted responsibility for our own problems and quit looking for someone to blame every time something goes wrong in our lives.

Adam and Eve were pretty good at playing the blame game, too. When God confronted them with their disobedience, Adam blamed Eve. Not to be outdone, Eve blamed the serpent. Nine of the best words you'll ever say are actually the most difficult: "I was wrong. I am sorry. Please forgive me." Try saying those words to God today.

Day 5
Matthew 4:1-11

Temptation is a universal issue. Even Jesus had to face it. He never sinned, but he did face temptation. After you've read today's verses, compare the temptations of Jesus with the temptations placed before Eve in Genesis 3:1-7. Write your thoughts about each temptation as you journal.

Do you see a common thread? Satan has always enjoyed tempting people with physical pleasure. He loves to offer people the possibility of becoming important or popular. He keeps doing it because almost all of us will fall for these temptations.

What temptations have been placed in front of you lately?

Read what Paul said about temptation: "No temptation has seized you except what is common to man. And God is faithful; he will not let you be tempted beyond what you can bear. But when you are tempted, he will also provide a way out so that you can stand up under it" (1 Corinthians 10:13).

How could this promise help you overcome temptation?

Ask God to help you find his way out when you're tempted.

WEEK 4
CAIN AND ABEL: UNACCEPTABLE SACRIFICE

MEMORY VERSE

"If you do what is right, will you not be accepted? But if you do not do what is right, sin is crouching at your door; it desires to have you, but you must master it." (Genesis 4:7)

INTRODUCTION

How can siblings be so different? Brothers and sisters can look different, act different, have different interests, and like different subjects in school. Even twins can be as different as night and day.

If you have brothers and sisters, what are some ways you're different? What are some ways you're alike?

Cain and Abel were brothers, but were they ever different! Abel was a shepherd, and Cain was a farmer. Abel was the younger child, and Cain was the older. Abel was a giving person, as demonstrated by his gift to God. Cain was a little on the cheap side. Can you see trouble brewing?

The story of Cain and Abel is a sad story because it ends with Cain killing his brother out of jealousy. Cain and Abel both presented gifts to God. God accepted Abel's offering, but he rejected Cain's. To make matters worse, the problem wasn't the lavish nature of Abel's gift to God. The problem was the stinginess of Cain's gift. Cain's inadequacy was his own fault.

Aren't we guilty of the same sin? We can be jealous of what others have or what they accomplish, when the real problem is our own laziness or lack of concern. At times our jealousy is even aimed at our own siblings.

As we begin this week's study, take inventory of your heart. Is there jealousy? If so, toward whom is that jealousy directed? What steps can you take this week to keep jealousy from getting a grip on you as it did on Cain? Allow God to speak to you as you look at the tragic experience of two brothers.

DAILY DEVOTIONS

Day 1
Genesis 4:1-5

A lot of teenagers are convinced their parents play favorites. I used to get so mad when I felt my parents were favoring one of my brothers over me. I never knew who I was more frustrated with—my parents or the sibling who was getting their attention.

That's the way Cain felt. It was bad enough that God rejected his offering. But God accepted his brother's offering. Cain's problem wasn't Abel. And the problem certainly wasn't God. The real problem was Cain's selfish spirit.

Do you ever deal with jealousy at home? If so, how do you deal with it?

Where else do you find jealousy creeping into the back of your mind? At school? On your job? On your sports team? Make some notes as you journal.

What are some healthy ways of dealing with feelings of jealousy whenever they crop up?

Pray this week that God will reveal any jealousy in your heart. Ask God to help you grow in your faith as a way to combat a jealous spirit.

Day 2
1 Corinthians 3:1-4

The new Christians in Corinth—one of the most important trade centers in ancient Greece—faced many problems. For one, their city was full of immoral behavior and false religions. In today's passage, Paul told these believers they needed to grow up spiritually. They were jealous of each other. Paul said this problem grew from their immaturity in Christ.

How is immaturity related to jealousy? Make some notes as you journal.

In your prayer time today, ask God to show you areas of your faith in which you need to mature. Then ask him to show you the first step in growing in your faith.

Day 3
1 Corinthians 5:9-13

This week you learned that Cain had a problem with jealousy. The Christians in Corinth also had a problem with jealousy. Paul told them it was because they were controlled by their own desires. They weren't acting very Christlike.

A mature faith is the best medicine for jealousy, so how can you—a student—take faith to a higher level? Paul says we should be careful about associating with Christians who don't live out their faith. Those people will zap our faith, not inspire it.

Is there anyone you spend time with who encourages you to stay immature in your faith? Think about the question and make some notes as you journal.

How can you distance yourself from people who are hurting your spiritual growth?

Day 4
Genesis 4:6-8

Cain had every opportunity to make things right with God. In fact, God spelled it out for him very clearly. What two things did God say sin would do in Cain's life?

What did God tell Cain about how to handle sin?

Cain didn't subdue his sin. Instead, it wound up destroying him and eventually led to the death of his brother. Sin is a big deal to God. It probably won't lead to killing your brother. However, when Satan tempts you to sin, his goal is to destroy your life. Sin may often seem harmless, but it always has consequences.

Allow God to reveal to you specific areas of sin in your life. They may be attitudes toward people, things you do when no one else is looking, or little areas of compromise in your life. Spend a few minutes talking to God about those areas of sin that he shows you. Ask him to forgive you of specific sins in your life.

Day 5
Genesis 4:9-16

Cain brought an inadequate offering to God. When God didn't accept it, Cain's heart became jealous. He wouldn't repent of his sin; he wouldn't set things right with God. He became bitter, and his bitterness soon turned into action. Cain killed his brother. The consequences of Cain's sin were almost too much for him to bear.

Sin—any sin—always carries consequences. Be thankful that God is a loving God and will forgive your sin anytime you ask him. Remember that the consequences will still be present, but the sin can be forgiven.

Can you think of a time when your sin caused serious consequences for you? If so, write about it as you journal.

Thank God that he'll always forgive your sin. Even if there may still be consequences for your actions, you can know God forgives.

WEEK 5
THE FLOOD

MEMORY VERSE

"By faith Noah, when warned about things not yet seen, in holy fear built an ark to save his family. By his faith he condemned the world and became heir of the righteousness that comes by faith." (Hebrews 11:7)

INTRODUCTION

In Noah's day the people were so wicked even their thoughts were totally evil. When God looked out over his creation, he was sorry he'd made people. Then as God looked out over the earth, he saw one righteous man, by the name of Noah, who'd trusted God for 500 years.

When God called Noah to build the ark, Noah accepted the task and spent the next 120 years working on the project. Imagine—120 years! Since Noah and his family were the only righteous people on earth, he probably worked on the ark while his neighbors gave him a hard time. The loneliness of the job must have been almost unbearable at times, but Noah was faithful to complete the project, and God saved his family from the flood.

If you feel as though you're the only one living for God at your school, on your team, or in your home, then it may be easy for you to relate to Noah. And like Noah, God is calling you to be a light for him in those places where evil has taken root. It may be tough to stand for God when no one else seems to, but you can do it if you trust God's power. Just remember that Noah carried God's light for 120 years.

DAILY DEVOTIONS

Day 1
Genesis 6:1-8

One Wednesday night our students were having a discussion about parental discipline. Several students mentioned things their parents do to them that they really hate. Then one of the guys told me the worst thing his parents could do to him was say they were disappointed in him. He loved his parents, and he hated the thought that he might do something to break their hearts.

We all sin. We all fail God. However, I've known people who seem to use that as an excuse to do things that break the heart of God. Real obedience to God isn't about fear of what he'll do; it's about loving God so deeply that you fear disappointing him.

How do you feel about the idea that your sin could break God's heart? As you journal, make a few notes about that.

Pray this week that the way you live your life will bring joy to the heart of your heavenly Father.

Day 2
Genesis 6:9-13

I once saw a high school yearbook with a picture of the school mascot on its cover. On closer examination, I realized the image was actually a compilation of small headshots of each senior at the school. In other words, a small photo of each senior was essential to make the bigger picture.

If we could somehow take a picture of God's plan for all humanity, a closer examination of that picture would reveal millions of tiny pictures of those who've followed God. One small picture would be of you. But each picture would be essential to make up the big picture.

Just as Noah was essential to God's restoring his plan on earth, you're an important part of God's work in this world.

What does your small picture within the big picture look like?

Pray that you'll do what you need to in order to play your part in the big picture of God's work.

Day 3
Genesis 6:14-22

No doubt about it, God gave Noah an incredible job. The ark took 120 years to build, and the finished product was a little bigger than a football field. Notice that God provided Noah with everything he needed to get the job done.

Whether it's a Noah-sized task or something smaller, always remember this: God will always provide everything you need to complete the job he calls you to do. He'll provide the resources, the wisdom, and his guidance through the Holy Spirit.

What is God calling you to do right now where you live?

What resources has he given you to get the job done?

Pray that God will give you eyes to see the tasks he's calling you to do.

Day 4
Genesis 8:1-19

We don't get much snow in the southern United States. So on those rare occasions when winter weather sets in, the streets are blocked, stores may close, and the city comes to a halt. I usually have to stay indoors for a few days, and my inability to get out and go places can cause me to feel some serious cabin fever.

After 377 days in an ark with a bunch of smelly animals and seven family members, do you believe Noah experienced a little cabin fever? Even when the rain stopped and it looked okay to get out of the ark, Noah remained faithful and waited on God's timing.

Waiting for God's timing can be hard. Noah was waiting for God's timing to get out of the ark. You may be waiting for God's timing to finish high school, get a driver's license, or find the girl or guy who is "the one." Never forget that God's timing is best.

Do you feel as if you're waiting for God's timing in some aspect of your life?

Don't let impatience spoil the great plans God has in store for you.

Day 5
Genesis 9:8-17

A covenant is a binding agreement between two parties. The account of Noah and the great flood concludes with God's promise to never again destroy the earth with a flood. The Bible is filled with promises from God. In each one God is always willing to give his full commitment to us.

How willing are you to give your full commitment to God?

If you're ready, write out a full commitment of your life to God as you journal.

WEEK 6
JOB: GOD'S PROVEN CONTROL

MEMORY VERSE

"Naked I came from my mother's womb, and naked I will depart. The Lord gave and the Lord has taken away; may the name of the Lord be praised." (Job 1:21)

INTRODUCTION

Have you ever had someone treat you as if you had no clue what you were doing? It's frustrating to deal with people who think they know it all. Job thought he had all the answers until he met the One who created the questions: God.

Satan was convinced Job wouldn't be as devoted to God if his possessions were taken away. God allowed Satan to test Job. Job lost his livestock, most of his workers, and his 10 children. He was struck with terrible boils. Suffering and grieving, Job wanted to know what was going on in his life.

Job pointed out his good character as if he were testifying in court. Then a surprise witness appeared. God answered Job with questions of his own: "Where were you when I laid the earth's foundation?" "Can you hold back the movements of the stars?" "Can you shout to the clouds and make it rain?"

Job got the message. He finally realized God was in control of everything. Job repented of his rebellion, and God eventually restored Job's fortune, doubling what he had before. God continued to bless Job throughout the rest of his life; but more importantly, Job learned some valuable lessons. He found out that living a life of obedience to God doesn't ensure a life without problems. Job also discovered that God knows and is concerned about everything that happens in the lives of his children.

DAILY DEVOTIONS

Day 1
Job 1:1-5

How would you define integrity? Job was described as a man of integrity because he feared God and stayed away from evil. In fact, Job was so intent on avoiding evil he even offered sacrifices on behalf of his children (just in case any of them had sinned and not sacrificed). If you want to be a person of godly integrity, then you'll have to distance yourself from sin and evil influences.

Do some personal evaluation today. In what ways are you like Job?

In what ways are you not like Job?

How diligent are you at keeping sin out of your life?

Pray this week that God will help you identify sinful situations and give you the courage to stay away from them.

Day 2
Job 1:6-12

Remember, Job didn't suffer because he was a bad person or because he'd done anything wrong. In fact, Job was a righteous man. As hard as it is to understand, Job suffered because he was a godly person.

Often we judge people who are suffering and assume they're somehow paying for some sin they've committed. For instance, we see a homeless man and assume he's in that situation because he can't stay away from alcohol.

Our sins will have consequences, and we often suffer because of our own sins. But we must remember that bad things do happen to good people. Yet in every situation, God is still in complete control.

Do you ever come to the conclusion that people who have problems in their lives are simply getting what they deserve? Instead, look at others—and yourself—through the perspective that maybe God isn't punishing them but building godliness into their lives.

Pray that through whatever pain you encounter, you'll seek to know and understand what God is teaching you.

Day 3
Job 2:1-10

When life is good and things are going well, we rarely stop and thank God for it. But just let something negative happen, and our first response is to cry out, "Why me, God?" But whether it's a good day, a bad day, or an average day, all days are under God's control. In fact, our very lives are in his hands. Think about this: If every aspect of your life were perfect, you wouldn't even realize how good life is because you'd have no bad times to compare it with. Look at the tough times as blessings, not as disappointments.

Thank God today for both your good and not-so-good experiences. Both are necessary for you to live and grow in godliness.

Day 4
Job 38:1-15

Do you believe God was mad at Job for asking all his questions? Someone once told me God never minds questions from an honest seeker. We can see here that Job discovered the wonder and power of God through his questions. If your desire is to know and understand the nature of God, then he welcomes all your questions. You don't have to fear going to God. You don't have to be concerned that God will become angry with you. He wants you to voice your hurts, your fears, and your problems.

Do you ever feel afraid to go to God with your questions?

Remember: God wants to hear from you.

In your prayer time today, be honest and ask God about the problems, fears, or trials you're facing.

Day 5
Job 42:1-5

Job said that what he'd known about God in the past (before his crisis) could be compared to only hearing about God. But as a result of his suffering, Job said he'd finally seen God.

In the lowest moments of life, God may reveal himself to you in amazing ways. If you're going through a tough time right now, don't give up on your faith. In the end you'll experience a closeness to God you never thought possible. When you're facing a crisis in your life, don't ignore God; increase your time in prayer all the more. You'll be surprised at the results. Your situation may not change, but God will draw close to you and walk with you through every difficulty.

Are you seeking God more today because of a problem in your life?

Pray that God will reveal himself to you, especially in times of difficulty.

WEEK 7
ABRAHAM: CHANNEL FOR BLESSING

MEMORY VERSE

"For he was looking forward to the city with foundations, whose architect and builder is God." (Hebrews 11:10)

INTRODUCTION

The life of Abraham (originally called Abram) and his place in Bible history are so important that we're going to spend three weeks examining his life. Abraham's story begins with his father moving the family from Ur to a village called Haran (Genesis 11:26-31). At the age of 75, Abraham answered the call of God and packed up his family to move to the land of Canaan.

Abraham lived in a time when people worshiped multiple gods. People believed certain gods looked out for their land and controlled things such as weather, health, and crops. It was common for people to believe that to move away from a region was to move away from the protection of the gods of that area. It took a lot of faith for Abraham to move his family, his servants, and all his possessions to a land in which he knew no one. He had to trust that the God who called him to move wasn't the God of only Haran, but also the God of Canaan and the whole world. The very act of moving showed that Abraham had placed his faith in the true God.

Abraham traveled with his nephew Lot. When trouble arose between Abraham's servants and those of Lot, Abraham offered Lot his choice of lands. Lot chose to inhabit the land close to the evil cities of Sodom and Gomorrah. Even though Lot chose the better land when he and Abraham parted ways, God still promised to give Abraham blessings beyond belief and a permanent home for him and his descendants. Abraham's life is a testimony to the fact that faith in God opens the door to God's blessings. That's what he promised Abraham, and God always keeps his promises.

DAILY DEVOTIONS

Day 1
Genesis 12:1-6

When I was in high school, my father took a job in a town two hours away. I wasn't crazy about leaving my hometown. If I'd been given a vote on this decision, I would have voted against it. Looking back, however, I can now see God's plan for me in that move. He provided a great church with a wonderful youth program, a good school with an active Christian club, and a girl who would eventually become my wife.

Making changes in life can be hard. When God calls you to do something different—change your friends, give up some hobby, or go to college across the country—it can take a lot of faith to obey. That's what's so amazing about Abraham. God told Abraham to go, and he went.

Pray this week that you'll be willing to follow God's call and direction for your life—wherever that leads.

Day 2
Genesis 12:7-9

A popular Christian writer refers to the habit of always looking at the negative side of things as "stinkin' thinkin'." If we have this mentality, we may hear God's call and then think only about how hard it is to be a Christian. God may ask us to do things that are hard, but that's far from the whole story. God pours incredible joy and blessing on those who are obedient to him.

One of the keys to Abraham's success, during his journey of more than 1,000 miles, was that he took time to worship God. It's really hard to focus on the negative when we're spending time thanking God and worshiping him. Worship is a wonderful cure for stinkin' thinkin'.

When are you most likely to fall into stinkin' thinkin'?

What do you do in private times of worship? Do you find those times change your attitude?

In your prayer time today, consider whether you're looking at your walk with Christ from an attitude of how much it costs you to follow him or how much he's blessed you. As you journal, list some of the things God has given you for which you can be thankful.

Day 3
Luke 5:27-32

God made a promise when he called Abraham to follow him. But sometimes God calls people without a specific promise, as in the case of Levi. Jesus said, "Follow me," and Levi followed Jesus. It's exciting to follow God out of simple obedience.

Does it excite you to know that your life can be an adventure of following God through obedience?

What's the most exciting part of obedience to God? As you journal make notes about how you feel about following God in obedience.

There's no telling what kinds of exciting things lie ahead for you. Pray that God will keep your heart open to what he may choose to do in your life.

Day 4
Genesis 13:10-13

We see it, it looks good, and we want it. Even though we follow God, it's sometimes tempting to be led by our eyes. Lot chose the best land when he and Abraham parted ways, but he certainly didn't choose the best company. The people in that land were unusually wicked, and their lifestyle eventually created havoc for Lot and his family.

Are there ways your eyes can get you off track? If so, what are they?

God has some great things in store for you, but you must allow him to lead you by your heart, not your eyes.

Day 5
Hebrews 11:8-10

In the movie *Star Wars*, Luke Skywalker tried to battle a probe with his light saber. After many unsuccessful attempts, his mentor challenged him to try the exercise without using his eyes—by pulling down the blast shield on his helmet. In other words, Luke was challenged to use his faith and not his sight.

Luke's faith in an unseen "force" was misplaced. God is so much more than an impersonal force—he relates to us in very personal ways. When we follow God, if we go only as far as we can see, then we'll never get where God wants to take us.

So pull down your blast shield and go on faith. You'll be amazed at what God will do in your life.

When have you acted on your simple faith in God? What was the result?

Why is it so much easier to trust what we can see?

Make some notes about what it will mean for you to start living more by faith.

Pray that God will grow your faith in him day by day.

WEEK 8
ABRAHAM: FAITH OR CONSEQUENCES

MEMORY VERSE

"Abram believed the Lord, and he credited it to him as righteousness."
(Genesis 15:6)

INTRODUCTION

The second part of Abraham's story is about the need for patience. God initiated a covenant with Abraham. (A covenant is a binding agreement between two parties.) God promised Abraham many blessings. God blessed Abraham with incredible wealth. The one big question Abraham had, however, was regarding God's promise of many descendants. As Abraham got older, he couldn't see that happening. In fact, Abraham even asked God what good all the blessings would be if he had no son to pass them on to.

Even though God assured Abraham and Sarah they'd have a son, they still took matters into their own hands. Abraham fathered a son with an Egyptian slave girl named Hagar.

Just think of the personal time and the intimate conversations God and Abraham shared. Think about the blessings and the promises God gave him—only to have Abraham doubt that God would give him a son by his wife Sarah.

God's promise would eventually be fulfilled in a miraculous way. When Abraham was 100 years old, his son Isaac was born.

Now more than ever, people want things immediately. Our temptation is to rush everything—including God. Patiently wait on God, and you'll see he always keeps his promises.

DAILY DEVOTIONS

Day 1
Galatians 3:6-9

Abraham was undoubtedly one of the most blessed people in the Bible. As Abraham placed his faith in God, God continued to add to Abraham's blessings.

In today's passage, Paul said we who put our trust in God can receive the blessings Abraham received. We might think of Abraham as some kind of superhuman. But God calls normal people to faith. God desires for his people to respond to him in faith. When they do, God loves to bless his people.

Can you identify ways in which God has already blessed you?

Pray today you'll learn to be aware of the blessings God sends your way.

Day 2
Genesis 15:1-7

I almost got in trouble for not reporting for jury duty. I had moved, the county hadn't received my new address, and I never received a notice. Judges don't look too fondly on people who don't show up for jury duty. Fortunately, when the clerk discovered they didn't have my correct address, the judge let me off the hook. I went from being in trouble to being in right standing with the judge. I don't think I'd have gone to jail for not showing up for jury duty, but it sure felt good to be forgiven.

Because of our sin, we're all guilty before God. All the good behavior in the world won't cause a person to be righteous in God's sight. When we've broken the Law in one place, the whole Law is broken. We can be forgiven only when God declares us forgiven, and God forgives us only when we respond to him in faith. God declared Abraham righteous—forgiven and in right standing with God—because of Abraham's faith.

How is your faith in God?

Can you trust God with anything? Or do you struggle with faith?

What could strengthen your faith?

As you journal, make some notes about the condition of your faith right now.

Day 3
Genesis 16:4-10

Once Abraham and Sarah decided to disobey God and came up with their own plan for a descendant, things got really bad. Abraham had a baby with Sarah's handmaiden, Hagar. Hagar had issues with Sarah, and Sarah got mad at Abraham. Then Sarah began mistreating Hagar with Abraham's consent, and Hagar decided to run away. It took an angel of the Lord to straighten out the whole mess. Conflict is going to happen when we replace God's plan with our plan.

Have you experienced conflict with your parents, your friends, or your church because you weren't following God's plans for you? What was that like?

Make a commitment today to be patient and to follow God. Not only is it the right thing to do, but it will also save you from a lot of pain.

Day 4
Genesis 21:1-7

A 100-year-old man fathers a son with a woman almost as old. That's pretty amazing—but God does some amazing things. In Jeremiah 32:27, God told the prophet, "I am the Lord, the God of all mankind. Is anything too hard for me?" The answer to that question would be a big "no"; nothing is too hard for God.

Have you seen God do anything totally amazing in your life? If so, what was it?

How different would your life be if you lived with Jeremiah 32:27 in mind?

As you pray today, ask God to show himself to you in big ways. Ask him to help you see how limitless he really is.

Day 5
Hebrews 11:11-12

God loves to turn the impossible into the possible. Physically, Abraham thought he and Sarah were too old to have a son, but God did the impossible and gave him Isaac.

You may have heard God call you to a specific task and thought you weren't talented enough, smart enough, or old enough to get the job done. What you believe is impossible is always possible when God is involved.

What's the biggest dream you have? Write some of your dreams as you journal.

Evaluate your dreams. Has God placed those dreams in your heart?

What dreams do you have that seem impossible? Could you see God fulfilling those dreams for you?

Ask God to make your dreams match his dreams for you. Trust that he'll do amazing things as you follow the dreams he gives you.

WEEK 9
ABRAHAM: THE EXTREME TEST

MEMORY VERSE

"By faith Abraham, when God tested him, offered Isaac as a sacrifice. He who had received the promises was about to sacrifice his one and only son." (Hebrews 11:17)

INTRODUCTION

When their son was born, Abraham and Sarah were so tickled they named him Isaac, which means "laughter." They were so happy. But one day, God told Abraham to sacrifice his son on an altar. Abraham's faith was about to be put to the supreme test. Remember, Abraham had doubted God's plan in the past. Would he follow God this time or do things his own way?

Abraham followed God's plan. He got up early, took Isaac and some servants to the land of Moriah, and prepared to offer his son on one of the mountains. An interesting bit of dialogue took place between Abraham and his two servants just before he took Isaac to the mountain. Abraham told them to wait while he and Isaac went a little farther: "We will worship and then we will come back to you" (Genesis 22:5). Did Abraham say "we" so he wouldn't upset Isaac? Or was Abraham's faith so great that he knew he wouldn't actually have to sacrifice his son? Or even if he did sacrifice Isaac, might Abraham have believed that God would raise Isaac from the dead? We don't know the answer to those questions, but we do know Abraham had the faith to be willing to do whatever God told him to do without question.

God tests our faith to prepare us for his purposes—both now and in the future. God won't test you in the same way he tested Abraham, but he'll test your faith to strengthen it.

DAILY DEVOTIONS

Day 1
Genesis 22:1-5

Math problems always look easy when a teacher works them on a board in the classroom. The rude awakening comes when a homework assignment forces you to hammer out the problems on your own. But all that homework probably helps in the long run. Try taking a math test without doing math homework, and you'll probably fail.

After promising Abraham that a great nation would be born of his son Isaac, God told Abraham to sacrifice his son. This test was probably meant to foreshadow what God would later do: Allow his own Son to die for the sins of the world.

God wants you to learn to trust him in every area of your life. Just as homework prepares you to take the test, God uses circumstances to test your faith and to prepare you for bigger challenges.

Is God testing you right now? If so, as you journal, make some notes about the test you're experiencing.

Pray you'll be faithful to learn what God wants to teach you through the experiences of your life.

Day 2
Matthew 19:16-22

The extreme test for the rich young man came in the form of a challenge. When Jesus told him that in order to inherit eternal life he must obey the commandments, he felt pretty good about himself. He'd been a commandment keeper. But the young man's face must have fallen when Jesus told him to give everything away. Giving away all he owned to the poor was more than this man could bear. After all, he was very rich. In the end his stuff was more important to him than a relationship with Jesus.

Take a survey of your life. What do you have that's more important to you than your relationship with Jesus? Sports? Members of the opposite sex? Your car? Make some notes as you journal.

If you have possessions more important to you than Jesus, ask yourself: Do you own them, or do they own you?

Day 3
Genesis 22:15-19

The final test for Abraham was whether or not he'd be willing to lay it all on the line for God. And he was willing to give up his most prized possession—his son Isaac—as a demonstration of his faith in God. That's total commitment.

Have you been reluctant to give up a week in the summer for a mission trip or unwilling to miss sleeping late on a Saturday morning to do a mission project? Those things seem small compared to what Abraham was willing to give up, but we all have to start our journey of faith where we are.

Are you ready to start giving total commitment to God? If not, why not?

Day 4
Romans 4:18-22

Football players usually spend quite a bit of time in the weight room. By getting stronger they become better athletes and are able to contribute more to their teams. God wants our faith strong. When Abraham was tested, his faith grew stronger, and this brought glory to God.

God is going to give you many opportunities to strengthen your faith. Maybe he's preparing you for the future or just helping you make a better contribution to the youth ministry at your church right now. Either way, be committed to strengthening your faith.

In what ways do you see God strengthening your faith in him?

How are you responding to God's work?

Day 5
James 2:21-23

Do you know someone famous? I wonder what it must be like for the guy who delivers groceries to the president of the United States. (I assume he has them delivered and doesn't just run down to the supermarket.) It would be pretty amazing to give the president and first lady their bologna and cheese, wouldn't it? In fact, I believe it's pretty impressive to hear someone talking about a well-known person and say, "That person is a friend of mine."

We probably look at fame the wrong way. I mean, you know the most famous person in the history of the universe—Jesus Christ. Isn't it awesome that you can say you know him? What an incredible experience you'll have one day when, because of your faith, Jesus looks at you face to face and calls you his friend. That'll top delivering bologna to the president any day.

Read verse 23 from today's passage one more time. What does the Bible mean when it calls Abraham "God's friend"?

What would it mean for you to be called God's friend? Make some notes as you journal.

WEEK 10
ISAAC AND REBEKAH

MEMORY VERSES

"Then the man bowed down and worshiped the Lord, saying, 'Praise be to the Lord, the God of my master Abraham, who has not abandoned his kindness and faithfulness to my master. As for me, the Lord has led me on the journey to the house of my master's relatives.'" (Genesis 24:26-27)

INTRODUCTION

The great story about the faith of Abraham continues in the life of his son Isaac. After Abraham's wife Sarah died, he was determined to find a good wife for his son. Convinced there were no suitable mates in the land of Canaan, Abraham sent a servant to Abraham's homeland of Haran to find a young woman who'd become Isaac's wife. The search was all about two things—faith and prayer.

Abraham sent his servant on the journey and told him God would send an angel ahead of him to help him. When the servant arrived at his destination, he took time to pray that God would give him success, and he asked for a sign to help him find the right woman. When the servant found Rebekah, he worshiped God and said a prayer of thanksgiving. When Rebekah's family gave her permission to marry Isaac, Abraham's servant again prayed and worshiped God.

The success of finding a wife for Isaac started with Abraham's incredible faith that God would bless him with many offspring. The servant completed his mission by praying over each decision. The final result was a thankful servant who was so overwhelmed by the goodness of God that his only response was worship.

If you choose to follow God, then he'll call you to faith and obedience. When you feel God calling you to a task, you should do as Abraham and his servant did:

1. *Begin with a strong faith.*
2. *Pray over each decision.*
3. *Acknowledge that your success comes from God.*
4. *Thank and worship God.*

DAILY DEVOTIONS

Day 1
Genesis 24:1-8

Have you given much thought to whom you'll one day marry? Outside your decision to become a Christian, that will be the most important decision you'll ever make.

Abraham believed God had a good wife for his son, and he acted in faith to make sure he found the right mate for Isaac. Your parents probably won't send out a servant to find you a future mate—at least, you're probably hoping they won't do that. Still, you can act on faith in the matter—right now.

What does God want for your relationship with your future mate?

What do you need to do now to prepare yourself for that future relationship?

Begin praying that God will send you the right person at the right time. If you're really bold, ask your parents to pray about this as well. Then wait to see what God will do.

Day 2
Genesis 24:12-14

Do you ever pray for success? Some television preachers would have you believe that God's will is for everyone to be rich and prosperous. But if you take one look at Jesus' bank account, then you know being financially rich isn't at the center of God's heart. But in this passage, the success Abraham's servant prayed for was to accomplish the purpose of his mission—to find the right wife for Isaac. In whatever God calls you to do, pray for God to give you success in accomplishing that task. God will always honor that unselfish prayer.

Is there a mission in some area of your life that you need to ask God to make successful? What is it?

Ask God to give you the ability to complete it successfully—for his glory.

Day 3
Genesis 24:15-22

Abraham's servant asked God for a specific sign in his search for a wife for Isaac. When Rebekah offered to give water to the servant and to his camels, he knew he'd found God's mate for Isaac.

One of the ways God can speak to us is through the circumstances we encounter. You may sense you should be helping more in your church, when the vacation Bible school director suddenly asks you to help with recreation for the children. Wham! That could well be God speaking to you.

But be careful: Not every circumstance is a word from God. Unlike Abraham's servant, you have God's Word—the Bible. Compare the circumstances you encounter with what the Bible says. Ask your parents or your pastor for godly counsel. But don't ignore what's happening around you. God will often use circumstances to reveal to you where he's working and what he wants you to do.

What do you see happening around you right now that could be an indication of something God wants you to do?

How can you compare that circumstance to God's Word?

Day 4
Genesis 24:48-51

I knew God was calling me into the ministry, but I was unsure what my college major should be. My uncle, who is a pastor, took me to three respected pastors. He guided me to ask each of these wise men for their counsel about what I should do. By the end of the day, I knew exactly what major to work toward in college.

Godly counsel can make a tremendous difference in your life. A pastor, a youth minister, a teacher, or a parent could be the person God has chosen to give you the words of wisdom you need in your walk of faith.

It was the same way for Abraham's servant. He knew the words of Rebekah's relatives would point him to the next step in his journey.

Is there an area of your life right now in which you need the advice of another person? If so, what is it?

Who is a person you respect and from whom you could seek godly counsel?

Day 5
Psalm 92:1-8

When Abraham's servant realized his search for a wife for Isaac was over, his first response was to worship God. He'd watched God guide his entire journey. The result of his obedience to God was the successful completion of a huge undertaking. How could he do anything but celebrate all God had done?

Notice how the psalmist in today's passage expressed joy. No matter where you are in your walk of faith, it's always a good thing to stop and give thanks to God for what he's done in your life.

As you journal, write down 10 things you're thankful for.

Write a prayer of thanksgiving to God. Let God know how thankful you are for what he has done and for what God is doing in your life.

WEEK 11
ISAAC: JACOB'S BLESSING

MEMORY VERSE

"And we know that in all things God works for the good of those who love him, who have been called according to his purpose." (Romans 8:28)

INTRODUCTION

Remember how the differences between Cain and Abel led to conflict and eventually Abel's death? The story of Isaac's twin sons, Jacob and Esau, is similar—and almost ended the same way.

The struggle between Jacob and Esau began while they were still in their mother's womb. God said this was a sign that the boys' descendants would become rival nations. This rivalry was clear as they grew older, partly because of the differences between the two. Esau was an outdoorsman; Jacob preferred staying inside. Esau's skin was rough; Jacob had smooth skin. Their father favored Esau; Jacob was favored by his mother.

The rivalry between the brothers grew when Jacob coerced Esau into trading his birthright for a bowl of stew. Things got worse when Jacob deceived his father into giving him a blessing meant for Esau. Esau then vowed he'd kill Jacob after Isaac died.

Much later in life, Jacob decided to try to make peace with his brother. They met after years of separation. But rather than try to kill his brother, Esau embraced Jacob and forgave him.

Looking at the two brothers, it'd be easy to assume God would use Esau to keep his promise to Abraham, right? Wrong. God honored Isaac's blessing of Jacob and used him to continue his great work of salvation. Even when God's ways don't seem to make sense, remember that his plans are perfect. God always knows what he's doing.

DAILY DEVOTIONS

Day 1
Genesis 25:19-23

Isaac did something very simple. He prayed and asked God for a child. God answered his prayer with two sons.

At my church, we discuss prayer requests almost every time we meet. We pray as if we expect God to answer, but we seldom discuss specific ways God has answered our prayers. Your church may do the same things. Sharing prayer requests is great, but we should also celebrate when God answers our prayers.

Write some specific things you're praying for right now. Leave some space to write God's answer to your prayers.

Be sure to come back to this space later and record God's answers. Remember that God may not always answer with a "yes." Sometimes he responds with an answer of "no" or "wait."

Day 2
Genesis 27:1-13

Tricking an old man isn't usually the way to find God's will. Nevertheless, that's exactly what Jacob did. He tricked his father, Isaac, into giving him the blessing he would have given to his older son, Esau. Jacob eventually paid for deceiving his father. (We'll look at that story next week.) Traditionally, the oldest son received the father's blessing, but God's will was for Jacob to be the link in his covenant with Abraham. God promised Abraham his descendants would become a great nation—that nation would come from Abraham's grandson Jacob. Sometimes the least likely person is the one through whom God chooses to do a great work.

Can you think of any situations in your life—or in the life of someone else—in which God worked through an unlikely situation or an unlikely person?

What lessons can you learn from situations like those?

Day 3
Ephesians 1:3-5

Passing on a blessing was a big theme in the Old Testament. Have you noticed all the stories about one person blessing another? Blessings were often passed on from father to son. Isaac was blessed by his father Abraham. Jacob received a blessing from his father Isaac.

Did you know you're blessed too? Read Ephesians 1:3 again. When you asked Jesus to be your Savior, you were blessed with every spiritual blessing in the heavenly realm. That's a lot of blessings.

What are your biggest blessings?

Take some time today to think about all the blessings God has given to you. As you journal, make some notes about them.

Don't forget to thank God for the blessings he gives you.

Day 4
Galatians 3:10-14

Do you ever daydream about receiving a large inheritance from some unknown relative? We can daydream all we want, but most of us will never be that fortunate. Still, material wealth is nothing compared with the spiritual blessings of God. God's blessings will last forever.

God's blessings are ours. They're available to us because we belong to God through Jesus. We don't receive these blessings because of our bloodline; we receive them because of our faith in Jesus Christ. Things in this life are temporary, but the blessings of God will last through eternity.

When you think of blessings from God, what do you include?

Do you tend to think mostly of physical blessings (like food and shelter) or spiritual blessings?

What do spiritual blessings from God look like?

The greatest blessing God has given you is the opportunity to spend eternity with him in heaven.

Day 5
Genesis 27:41-46

Jacob used deception to get his father's blessing, and then he had to live with the consequences of that deception. Jacob had to leave the country because his brother, Esau, vowed to kill him. Jacob wasn't much of an adventurer. He was more of a "mama's boy." To leave his parents, the familiar surroundings of his home, and the convenience of being the son of a prominent man must have been hard for Jacob.

God will forgive any sin, but the consequences of that sin may last a long time. It's been said that we're free to make our own choices, but we're not free to choose the consequences.

Can you think of some things you've done for which you asked forgiveness from God but are still paying the consequences?

Pray that God will help you avoid sins with difficult consequences.

WEEK 12
JACOB: ISRAEL'S FAMILY ROOTS

MEMORY VERSES

"Do not be deceived: God cannot be mocked. A man reaps what he sows. The one who sows to please his sinful nature, from that nature will reap destruction; the one who sows to please the Spirit, from the Spirit will reap eternal life." (Galatians 6:7-8)

INTRODUCTION

Jacob was on the run from Esau because he'd tricked his brother out of both his birthright and his father's blessing. One night, during his journey to his uncle Laban's house, Jacob had a dream. In it God reaffirmed his promise to bless Abraham through Jacob. Of course that meant Jacob would have many descendants, which also meant he'd be looking for a wife.

Later, Jacob was convinced Rachel, the beautiful daughter of his uncle Laban, was definitely the woman for him. For seven years Jacob worked for his uncle so he'd have the opportunity to marry Rachel. When the day of the wedding came, however, Laban didn't put Rachel behind the wedding veil. Instead, it was his older and less attractive daughter, Leah.

After tricking his brother out of their father's blessing, Jacob had been tricked. So he worked seven more years for the right to marry his beloved Rachel. Was God trying to teach Jacob a lesson by allowing the deceiver to be deceived? Probably. But God's perfect plan was the most important piece of this puzzle. The 12 sons of Jacob would eventually become the pillars of the new nation. And the children of Leah, not Rachel, represented the most influential groups.

God's ways and his timing are perfect. The great people of the Old Testament had to learn that lesson—and it's a lesson we're still learning today.

DAILY DEVOTIONS

Day 1
Genesis 28:10-15

Jacob must have been exhausted. Can you imagine using a rock for a pillow? When Jacob fell asleep, God spoke to him in a dream. Jacob saw a stairway leading to heaven, with angels going up to heaven and coming down to earth. The dream must have been an amazing picture. When God spoke to Jacob, he reaffirmed the promises he'd made to Jacob's grandfather, Abraham. God will always keep his promises.

God has made promises that apply to you as well. He's even given you a record of the promises he's made to those who follow Christ—the Bible. Pray today and thank God for the Scriptures.

What promises from the Bible are you claiming in your own life?

Make a commitment to spend more time reading the promises of God in your Bible. If you don't spend time with God and in the Bible each day, then you're neglecting a great treasure.

Day 2
Genesis 28:16-19

Read what Jacob said in verse 16 once more. Is it possible to be completely surrounded by the presence of God and not be aware of it? That happened to Jacob and it can happen to us as well. Whether you're at youth camp, a weekend conference, or church, or just hanging out with your friends in the youth group, the presence of God is there. Expect God to be with you, look for his presence, and experience it.

Have you ever been in a certain place or with a specific group of Christian friends when you thought, *I really feel the presence of God?* When was it? What was it like?

What brought about the strong feeling that God was present at that particular time?

Day 3
Genesis 28:20-22

After all Jacob and his relatives went through, Jacob still wanted proof before he'd accept Jehovah as his God. Amazing! But Jacob received proof from God.

God will make himself known to people. However, God is most honored when we act by faith, not by sight. Hebrews 11:6 states, "Without faith it is impossible to please God." God is pleased when we act out of obedience without asking for proof.

Search your heart. What do you believe God wants from your life? If you believe in your heart that God wants this from you, then what more do you need from God to pursue his purpose for you?

Spend a few minutes listening to God today. If you sense God speaking to you about something, write in this journal what you believe he's telling you.

Day 4
Genesis 29:20-27

A very important biblical principle plays out in these verses: You'll reap what you sow. Jacob deceived his brother, and then Jacob was deceived by his uncle. Your attitudes and actions are like planted seeds—one day you'll harvest the crop from those seeds. That harvest could be rich and rewarding, or it could be difficult and painful. It all depends on the kind of seeds you plant.

What seeds are you sowing in your life?

Considering your lifestyle now, are you concerned about what you'll reap in the future?

Ask God to help you live in a way that's pleasing to him so you'll reap a wonderful crop of benefits from the seeds you're sowing.

Day 5
Matthew 1:1-6

Apparently Jacob thought Rachel was gorgeous while Leah wasn't really all that attractive. But King David would be a descendant of Leah. In fact, even Jesus would be a descendant of Leah. Jacob was looking on the outside when he chose Rachel, but God knew what he planned to do when he chose Leah.

You may get caught up in society's way of believing that outward beauty is what's really important. But God doesn't define beauty as we do. If you're obedient to him, then you're truly beautiful.

Have you been guilty of judging others by their outward appearance?

Write the initials of someone you were wrong about in this area— someone who surprised you with inner beauty.

Do you judge your own worth by what you see in the mirror?

Few of us will ever look like the airbrushed models on magazine covers. Most of us don't look like finely toned athletes. But if God sees you as his unique creation, perhaps you shouldn't be too quick to judge what you see in the mirror.

WEEK 13
JACOB: DEALING WITH THE PAST

MEMORY VERSE

"So Jacob called the place Peniel, saying, 'It is because I saw God face to face, and yet my life was spared.'" (Genesis 32:30)

INTRODUCTION

Years ago every town had some kind of fix-it shop. But in the twenty-first century, those kinds of stores are about as rare as an eight-track tape. Today most of us simply throw away something broken and buy a new one. But what about a broken relationship? Should we try to fix it or just forget about it and move on?

The second part of Jacob's story is all about dealing with broken relationships. First he had to deal with his uncle Laban. After years of unfair treatment, Jacob left the land of his uncle under instructions from God. Laban wasn't happy about his daughters leaving, so he followed Jacob. Eventually Jacob and Laban made peace with each other after a face-to-face confrontation. Then Jacob dreaded the next encounter—the time had come to confront his brother, Esau.

By now, God had dealt with Jacob in many ways. Jacob wasn't the same young man who'd stolen his brother's birthright and blessing. A dream about a ladder to heaven, years spent working for his uncle, and a wrestling match with an angel had helped to strengthen both Jacob's character and his faith.

When he met Esau, Jacob bowed in submission. Then Jacob and Esau embraced each other in tears. God had changed the hearts of both men, and they reconciled.

Jacob's life is a testimony to the fact that fractured relationships can be fixed. God is the great Healer, and he may be at work healing your broken relationships right now. The first step in the healing process could be letting God change you as he did Jacob.

DAILY DEVOTIONS

Day 1
Genesis 31:38-42

Noah found it. Abraham found it. Job found it. Now it was Jacob's opportunity to find it as well. What each man discovered was the awe-inspiring grace of God in the midst of trouble and hardship. Jacob's father-in-law, Laban, had coerced Jacob to labor for him for 14 years in order to marry his daughters. As he confronted Laban, Jacob spoke clearly about the way he'd seen God work in his own life.

Something about hard times can allow us to see God clearly—if we're willing to look for him. If you're experiencing tough times, then you're also on the verge of discovering God's love in a powerful way.

Are you facing a difficult time? If so, what is it? (You may have more than one.)

Have you taken that difficult time to God, asked for his help, and given this worry to him? Make some notes as you journal.

Pray that God will give you the spiritual insight to see how he's at work in your life. Pray the difficult times you face will cause you to draw closer to him.

Day 2
Romans 8:26-30

Think about the interactions between our solar system, people, nature, technology, and governments in the world each day. As complex as they are, God is still able to work all things together for your good. That's mind-boggling and amazing. But he's a mind-boggling and amazing God.

Are you facing something right now that you just can't imagine will ever be worked out?

If you aren't facing anything like that now, you will someday. Allow God to have such an important part in your life that you couldn't imagine making it through a problem without him. God wants your relationship with him to be like that.

Day 3
Genesis 32:24-30

We all wrestle with things in life. Jacob physically wrestled with an angel. As a result, his name was changed to Israel, which means "one who struggles with God." Struggles in life make us stronger. Struggles with our faith make us spiritually stronger.

If you're honest, you'll admit your first instinct is to see all struggles from a negative perspective. Only by looking at the negatives from God's perspective can we change our own perspective. Thank God today for the opportunity to grow in your faith as a result of your struggles.

How do you view your struggles? Are you able to see their positive potential when you're going through them? Write your thoughts as you journal.

Ask God to help you see your struggles through his eyes.

Day 4
Genesis 35:1-3

A friend who'll stick by you in both good and bad times is a true friend. Jacob realized God was the real thing because God answered Jacob's prayer by staying by his side in all situations. In today's passage, Jacob heard from God and then he obeyed.

No matter what happens to you in life—and no matter how you feel— God is always right beside you. His Holy Spirit will never leave you. You can't trust your feelings; feelings will lie to you. You can't trust the "foreign gods" of money, looks, fame, athletic ability, or affections from the opposite sex. All these will either leave you or deceive you. But you can always trust God. An old hymn says it best: "Trust and obey."

Do you trust God enough to be obedient to him? If not, why not?

What changes would you have to make to be able to do this?

God is waiting for you.

Day 5
Genesis 35:9-15

In verse 11 of this passage, God told Jacob he is God Almighty. Everything he promised Jacob came true.

Sometimes life can seem overwhelming—and maybe even unbearable—but just keep in mind that God is God Almighty. He's bigger than anything you'll ever face and is more than able to keep promises. God is the same God to us that he was to Jacob.

Are there areas of your life in which you're not totally trusting God?

What will it take for you to learn to trust God in everything?

WEEK 14
JOSEPH: DEALING WITH REJECTION

MEMORY VERSE

"You intended to harm me, but God intended it for good to accomplish what is now being done, the saving of many lives." (Genesis 50:20)

INTRODUCTION

I recently asked a group of students if any of them felt as though their parents favored a brother or sister over them. They all said "yes." These teenagers' feelings may not have been justified, but Joseph's father did favor Joseph over his brothers. Joseph was the darling of the family.

Joseph's parents treated him as if he were special for many reasons. He was the first child Jacob had by his beloved second wife, Rachel. Joseph was younger than most of his siblings. In fact, until his younger brother Benjamin was born, he was the baby of the family for 12 years. Then right after the birth of Benjamin, Rachel died. So Joseph was one of only two remaining links to Rachel that Jacob still had.

The relationship between Joseph and his brothers was tense. The tension got worse when Jacob presented his favored son with a beautiful, richly ornamented robe. Not long after that, Joseph had a dream about 12 bundles of grain, one representing each brother. He told his brothers that in his dream their bundles of grain bowed down to his bundle. They understood what Joseph meant: They'd bow to him even though they were his older brothers.

That did it. They found an opportunity to sell Joseph to some Ishmaelite traders, and then they told Jacob that wild animals had killed his son.

Joseph spent the next 13 years either working as a slave for Potiphar or serving time in prison. But during those years, Joseph experienced God's love and protection in powerful ways. God had big plans for Joseph—just as he has big plans for you.

DAILY DEVOTIONS

Day 1
Genesis 37:2-11

Something was special about Joseph. His father loved him a little more than he loved his other sons, and he didn't even try to hide it. Did you notice the special gift Jacob gave to his son Joseph?

But something else was special about Joseph: God had his hand on him in a unique way. Joseph's dreams were real. God really did plan to lift Joseph up later in life, and his brothers really would bow down to him. Joseph knew he was special—and he let his brothers know it, too.

You're probably really good at something. You may even be good at lots of things. Do you talk with others about your abilities? Do you let them know how good you are? Or do you discount your own gifts as if they're not that big a deal? God doesn't gift us so we can brag about it, nor does he expect us to downplay the gifts he's given us. Rather, he leads us to give all the glory to him for his gifts.

Do you know what spiritual gifts and natural abilities you have? What are they?

How do you talk about your abilities with others?

Do you acknowledge God as the One who made you special?

Pray that God would help you to give him the glory for the gifts he's given to you.

Day 2
Genesis 37:18-28

Joseph's brothers didn't want to be guilty of killing him, so they decided to sell him as a slave instead. That doesn't make much sense, does it? Joseph's brothers didn't mind feeling some guilt, just as long as it wasn't a really high degree of guilt. They wouldn't kill Joseph, but they were satisfied with just getting him out of the way by selling him into slavery.

Feelings of guilt aren't necessarily bad things. Some people feel guilty when they haven't done anything wrong—that's a problem. But most of the time, when we feel guilty it's because we are guilty. Feelings of guilt can be a warning that we're not following God's plan. The good news is God never intends for us to live with guilty feelings. He's willing to forgive us any sin.

When do you feel guilty?

What do you do when you feel guilty? Do you dismiss the feeling or make it right with God (and with anyone else you've wronged)?

Ask God to help you to keep your heart right with him and with other people. Ask him for forgiveness for any sins you've committed. If you've hurt someone else, ask for that person's forgiveness as well.

Day 3
Psalm 18:25-30

This psalm was written by King David, but it sounds like something Joseph could have written. Both David and Joseph discovered that God's ways are perfect and that his promises are true. Joseph, like David, often depended on God's shield of protection. Neither one of these men of God could have made it through their circumstances without God.

Are you in a tough situation at home or at school? What is it?

Things may not be easy right now, but God promises never to leave us or forsake us (Deuteronomy 31:6).

Pray today and ask God to be your shield of protection in all situations.

Day 4
Jeremiah 9:23-24

Joseph had a tendency to brag about the special treatment he received from his father. Bragging is a sign of immaturity—and Joseph eventually learned his lesson the hard way. Jeremiah said if you want to brag about something, then brag about the fact that you delight in the knowledge of God.

Do you tend to make sure others know about one of your abilities? Remember that God gave this ability to you. We should reflect his glory, not our own.

Day 5
Genesis 50:14-21

Joseph's brothers sold him into slavery, and he served as a slave until he was falsely accused of attempted rape by his master's wife. Then he was sent to jail. By the grace of God, Joseph rose to a high place in Pharaoh's service, but Joseph had years of difficulty to endure—and all because of his brothers. How could Joseph ever forgive them?

Joseph was able to forgive his brothers because he believed God was in control. Joseph believed everything that had happened to him was part of God's plan. And Joseph's forgiveness demonstrated to his brothers the love of God.

On Day 2, we discussed your need to ask for forgiveness or to make something right with someone you'd wronged. But do you need to forgive someone who's wronged you?

Who is it?

Your act of forgiveness will be a demonstration of God's love that could change not only your attitude, but also your life.

WEEK 15
JOSEPH: REFUSING TEMPTATION

MEMORY VERSE

"No temptation has seized you except what is common to man. And God is faithful; he will not let you be tempted beyond what you can bear. But when you are tempted, he will also provide a way out so that you can stand up under it." (1 Corinthians 10:13)

INTRODUCTION

Life is like a roller coaster ride. It's full of ups and downs. Joseph experienced that roller coaster ride in a big way. He was treated as the favored son and then sold into slavery. He rose from the lowest of servants in Potiphar's house to supervisor over everything. Then he ended up in jail.

Joseph was actually thrown in prison for the crime of resisting temptation. Potiphar's wife tried again and again to seduce Joseph, but he was able to keep from sinning. How?

- *He loved and feared the Lord.*
- *He respected his master, Potiphar.*
- *He ran away from the temptation.*

You can't avoid life on a roller coaster. You're surrounded by friends one day, but you feel all alone the next. You scored the winning touchdown last week, but you fumbled the ball three times this week. And if your parents divorce or move to another city, then life can feel totally out of control.

But you can control the turmoil created when you give in to temptation. Follow Joseph's lead: Resist sin by loving and fearing God, respecting other people, and choosing to avoid—or even run away from—the situation if you must. Just remember the acronym FLEE (Fear the Lord; Escape Enticement).

DAILY DEVOTIONS

Day 1
Genesis 39:6-9

God told Adam and Eve they could eat anything in the garden except the fruit from one tree. Potiphar gave Joseph access to everything in his home except his wife. Adam and Eve suffered for their decision to disobey God. Oddly enough, Joseph also suffered as a result of his decision to do the right thing. The difference was that Adam and Eve gave in to temptation, and Joseph was able to resist it. Joseph put his love for God and his respect for his master above the possible pleasure the temptation held.

Are you being lured by any specific temptation at this point in your life? If you're not, then you will be. You probably already know the areas of sin in which you're most tempted. Be prepared by deciding right now that you'll not give in to those temptations when they come your way. Don't wait until you're faced with temptation to decide what to do; if you do, then temptation will be that much harder to resist.

Use your journal to write a commitment to God about how you'll face future temptations.

Ask God to help you have the same strength Joseph had whenever you face temptations in your life.

Day 2
Genesis 39:10-15

You know what peer pressure is all about, so consider how Joseph felt when Potiphar's wife approached him every day with the temptation to sin. He found that the best thing to do was to stay away from her as much as possible. If you're facing any type of temptation, the difference between giving in and resisting may be found in the amount of distance you put between yourself and the situation.

If something tempts you to sin, then stay away from it. Why make things harder by seeing how close you can get to sin? Make it easier on yourself by avoiding the situation completely.

Ask God for his help and protection from the temptations you face.

Day 3
Matthew 6:9-15

The Lord's Prayer includes a passage about temptation. Temptation is a pretty serious thing if Jesus (who never sinned) prayed about it. Not only are we to pray for help in resisting sin, but Jesus also reminded us that the person behind temptation is the evil one—Satan. The next time you're tempted, remember who your enemy is: Satan.

Have you ever realized that when you give in to temptation, you're actually pleasing Satan?

That sounds horrible, but it's the truth. Every time you're faced with a temptation and you willingly choose to give in, you're choosing Satan over God. What a terrible choice!

Ask God for the strength to always choose him and his ways over the ways of the deceiver.

Day 4
James 1:12-18

Satan knows your weak spots, and he tempts you with the things that appeal to your desires. But as you grow in faith, your desires will be replaced with godly desires. The more time you spend with God, the more your heart will desire the same things God desires for you. And that process gives Satan less ammunition with which to tempt you.

Satan will always look for your weaknesses, and you'll always have to stay close to God if you want to avoid sin. But you can resist temptation by filling your life with the things of God.

What are you filling your life with?

Pray about consciously choosing God more and more so your temptations will become fewer and fewer.

Day 5
Genesis 39:19-23

Joseph resisted temptation, and his great reward was—the opportunity to spend a couple of years in jail. While that seems so unfair, the bottom line in Joseph's life was that God was pleased with him. And God was preparing to bless Joseph in a tremendous way. Resisting sin may not result in immediate benefits every time, but God uses each instance of overcoming a temptation to make us a little more like him. And don't worry—positive results will eventually happen.

Don't be discouraged. Sometimes doing the right thing isn't easy. Sometimes it's even painful. But as you obey God's commands, you're becoming more of the person he wants you to be.

Think about your biggest areas of temptation. Are you standing against those temptations, or have you just allowed those sins to become a part of your lifestyle?

Use your journal to create a plan for staying in (or entering) the battle against temptation. What do you need to do?

Pray that God will give you strength to persevere in doing right—even when you don't see immediate results.

WEEK 16
JOSEPH: FROM PRISON TO PALACE

MEMORY VERSES

"Humble yourselves, therefore, under God's mighty hand, that he may lift you up in due time. Cast all your anxiety on him because he cares for you." (1 Peter 5:6-7)

INTRODUCTION

Helen Keller once said, "Character cannot be developed in ease and quiet. Only through experience of trial and suffering can the soul be strengthened, vision cleared, ambition inspired, and success achieved." The whole time Joseph was going from places of honor to places of dishonor, God was using those experiences to strengthen Joseph's character so he could one day manage the food supply for an entire nation. God's ultimate purpose was to save his chosen people from starvation.

Joseph was truly blessed by God. Things worked out well for him personally because he was appointed second in command under Pharaoh. God blessed Joseph in his finances, and he became a very wealthy individual. He was given nice clothes, use of the company chariot, and the opportunity to marry the Pharaoh's own daughter. On the spiritual side, God used Joseph to preserve the lives of his chosen people—the Hebrew nation. As we come to the end of the story about Joseph's life, do you believe Joseph could say all things had worked together for good?

The story of Joseph is one of the great stories in the Bible. Because of Joseph's faith in God and his unwavering ability to trust God in very difficult circumstances, God's will was done and his people were saved.

As with Joseph, God is working on your character. Each day things will come your way that will shape your tomorrow. Some days will be difficult; others will be full of joy. Some days will give you the opportunity to make a difference in someone else's life; others will involve others investing in you. Always remember Romans 8:28—in all things God works for the good of those who love him.

DAILY DEVOTIONS

Day 1
Genesis 39:19-23

Joseph was thrown into jail knowing he was completely innocent. He was in a foreign land. He didn't have a friend to offer help. He was lost—except for God. Joseph was a capable person, but it wasn't his abilities that allowed him to gain favor. It was the work of God in his life. It would have been so easy for Joseph to get angry and become violent and abusive. But Joseph calmly submitted to the purposes of God.

You'll also face situations that are unfair. But those situations have a way of revealing your character. When things seem unfair, trust that God is in control.

How do you handle situations in which you're treated unfairly?

How does the way you handle those situations reveal your character?

What would it take for you to trust God in those situations?

Day 2
Genesis 40:8-15

Most colleges start the first classes of the semester with stern discussions about plagiarism. Professors threaten freshmen with expulsion for stealing someone else's work and taking credit for themselves. With Internet access, it can be pretty tempting to claim someone else's work as your own. If it's wrong to steal credit for what another person did, then how much worse would it be to take credit for what God has done?

Even though he was good at what he did, Joseph quickly pointed out that interpreting dreams was God's business. Joseph was acknowledging that God was behind the scenes in every phase of his life.

To whom do you give credit for your God-given abilities? Do you claim credit or do you give God the glory for them?

Day 3
Genesis 41:14-32

When it came time to interpret a dream for Pharaoh, Joseph knew he was in way over his head. Joseph told Pharaoh that God and only God had the power to do such a thing. The power to do the impossible can come from only one source: God. Are you plugged in to that power?

God will give you the ability to do whatever you need to do. He'll supply the strength or wisdom you need—right when you need it.

Are there things you feel you won't be able to do—either now or in the future? What are they?

Ask God to show you how to trust him to do amazing things in your life.

Day 4
John 15:1-8

Joseph knew God was the source of all his abilities. Much later, Jesus told his disciples they could do nothing without him. Jesus wanted his followers to realize they were totally dependent upon God for everything.

You may feel you're strong enough or smart enough to get through life on your own. But sooner or later, everyone confronts situations beyond their abilities. Everyone needs God—whether or not they acknowledge that need. Learn to draw on God's strength and wisdom now. As you learn to depend on him, you'll find he's always there when you need him. Life won't always be easy, but God will help you bear the load.

Are you depending on God in every decision—or do you seldom feel the need to rely upon God?

God wants us to depend on him like we depend on our next breath of air.

Day 5

Genesis 45:3-8

As Joseph looked back on his life, he understood that the major events in his life—being sold into slavery, being falsely accused and placed in prison, interpreting the dreams of his fellow prisoners and later the dreams of Pharaoh, rising to a place of honor in Egypt—had all happened for a particular reason. He could honestly tell his brothers that everything in his life had happened so he could save their lives.

While you're going through difficult circumstances, the situation may not make any sense. But when you look back at the things that have happened to you, you'll see that the pieces of your life fit together like the pieces of a puzzle.

What's the moral of the story? Be patient and let God do his work. In the end you'll be able to see how God worked in each situation for your good and to accomplish his will.

Are you going through something difficult right now—and there seems to be no reason for it? What's the situation?

Just wait on God—you may not be able to be glad about the difficulty now, but one day you'll most likely look back and see what a blessing it was.

WEEK 17
MOSES: SENT BY GOD, RELUCTANT TO GO

MEMORY VERSE

"But he said to me, 'My grace is sufficient for you, for my power is made perfect in weakness.' Therefore I will boast all the more gladly about my weaknesses, so that Christ's power may rest on me." (2 Corinthians 12:9)

INTRODUCTION

When the book of Genesis ended, the Hebrew people were living the good life in Egypt. Now the book of Exodus opens with them working as Egyptian slaves. So what happened during the 400 years between the two books? An Egyptian regime came into power that didn't recognize the importance of the Hebrews. In fact, the new Pharaoh enslaved God's people and used them for cheap labor. He also ordered all male Hebrew children to be killed in an effort to slow down their explosive population growth.

This is the world into which Moses was born. Jochebed—his mother—didn't want her baby to die, so she hid Moses in a basket in the brush. Then one of Pharaoh's daughters found Moses and adopted him as her own child.

Moses grew up as a prince of Egypt. But after years of living in privilege, Moses killed an Egyptian and fled both his lavish lifestyle and his homeland. His journey took him to Midian, where he married and settled into the life of a shepherd.

The life of a nomad might have been fine for some people, but not for a man with a call of God on his life. God spoke to Moses through a burning bush and told him he'd lead the Hebrew people out of captivity and into the Promised Land. With much reluctance and very little faith, Moses accepted the challenge and obeyed God. That simple act of saying "yes" to God started one of the most amazing human transformations ever recorded in the Bible.

DAILY DEVOTIONS

Day 1
Exodus 3:1-6

Moses' journey of faith started with God getting his attention. God is pursuing you and working to get your attention, too. No, don't go looking for a burning bush, because God probably won't use one of those to get your attention. (However, he could if he wanted to.) Worship services at your church, Sunday school, discipleship classes, youth camps, mission trips, and day-to-day life experiences are just some of the avenues God uses to get you to open your spiritual eyes and see him at work.

In what ways is God trying to get your attention? Think about it and make some notes in your journal.

Pray this week that you'll allow God to get your attention.

Day 2
Exodus 3:7-17

It may seem like a strange question for Moses to ask God: "What is your name?" He may have asked this because each Egyptian god had a name. But the God of the Hebrews was simply their God.

Did you notice how God answered Moses? Read verse 14 again. The name God claimed for himself was "I AM." God wasn't a god who could be restricted to one area of life. He wasn't the god of the sun or the god of the harvest. No, God is the One who is and was and always will be. God is "I AM."

We try to restrict God today, too. We want God to be the God of Sunday morning, or the God of youth camp. That's not God. He's the God of every aspect of life. There are no parts of your life that have nothing to do with God.

Can you think of any areas of your life you've tried to separate from God?

Do you include God in your selection of friends, in your food choices, in the way you treat your parents, or in the way you handle your schoolwork?

Make some notes in your journal about the areas of your life you've tried to separate from God.

Day 3
Exodus 4:10-17

Jill Briscoe wrote a book titled *Here Am I—Send Aaron!* Sometimes when we hear God's call, we want to offer him a bunch of excuses because we feel inadequate. Moses certainly did. But that way of thinking is focused on self, not on God.

Never allow yourself to feel inadequate when God puts a task in front of you, because he always knows what he's doing; God will give you the ability to do it. Don't trust in yourself; trust in God.

Is there something God wants you to do but you haven't done it because you feel inadequate?

Make a commitment to turn that over to God and allow him to do his work through you.

Day 4
Hebrews 11:24-29

This passage from Hebrews offers a look back at the life of Moses. It took God a long time to get Moses to the place where he'd be considered one of the great men of faith in the Bible. But from where he began to where he finished, Moses grew by miles.

Today you may feel like a spiritual flop; but in racing terms, remember that the Christian life is a marathon—not a sprint. Each day is filled with struggles, but with each struggle God is perfecting your life.

When it comes to being faithful to what God has called you to do, do you feel as though you fail more than you succeed?

If you answered "yes," remember the life of Moses. He started out doubting God, but in the end he was known for his faithfulness.

Don't give up. Great things lie ahead for you if you keep the faith—and never give up on God.

Day 5
Psalm 25:1-10

Wouldn't it be great for God to reveal his will to you in an e-mail message? Knowing God's will means being in God's presence. Moses had clear verbal instructions from God, and he knew exactly what God's will was. Prayer is certainly a very important part of discerning the will of our Father because it draws us closer to him. The closer we are to God, the clearer his will becomes.

During your prayer time, have you ever felt God speak to you about something specific he wanted you to do?

Have you ever felt God speak to you through the advice or counsel of someone you trust?

Have you ever felt God leading you to do something specific as a result of reading his Word?

Don't place God in a box and believe he's limited to revealing his will to you in only one specific way. God may speak to you in a number of ways. However, be sure of this: If you want to hear from God, then you'll have to draw near to him.

Thank God for his desire to communicate his will to you—however he chooses to do so.

WEEK 18
MOSES: SPEAKING ON GOD'S BEHALF

MEMORY VERSE

"When Moses went and told the people all the Lord's words and laws, they responded with one voice, 'Everything the Lord has said we will do.'" (Exodus 24:3)

INTRODUCTION

Moses had been a shepherd for 40 years when God spoke to him through a burning bush and called him to lead the Hebrew people out of captivity. This job was going to require a lot of public speaking, and it's safe to say that four decades of talking to sheep out in the middle of nowhere did little to prepare Moses for the awesome task before him.

Moses was quick to point out all the reasons why God's plan to save the people of Israel wouldn't work. First, Moses told God he was just a nobody. Then Moses said the Hebrew people wouldn't believe he'd really spoken to God. Finally, he protested by saying he wasn't a good speaker. God answered each of Moses' concerns and assured Moses he was the person to get the job done.

Just think how excited Moses must have been when he went to visit Pharaoh. Any confidence he had, however, was quickly destroyed when Pharaoh—and then the Israelites—rejected him and the plan from God. Down and almost out, Moses went back to God and wanted to know why the job was so difficult.

Eventually, Moses became the man God knew he could be, and he led the Hebrews on an amazing journey from slavery to the Promised Land. Moses knew what God wanted him to do. Despite trouble of enormous proportions, Moses eventually completed the task. His success was ultimately due to his faith in God. You'll find success in the same way when God calls you to serve him.

DAILY DEVOTIONS

Day 1
Exodus 7:1-7

Moses had already been to Pharaoh once, and he'd said exactly what God told him to say. The result was rejection and an increased workload for the Hebrew slaves. Moses complained to God, "Since I speak with faltering lips, why would Pharaoh listen to me?" (Exodus 6:30). God's answer is found in today's verses. God told Moses to go back to Pharaoh because in the end, the people would realize he was the one true God. God told Moses to be persistent. Eventually, Moses' persistence paid off.

When you believe you're doing what God has led you to do, how persistent are you? How quickly do you give up?

Pray this week that God will help you be persistent in your walk with him. Don't give up; if God is in it, he'll work with you to complete the task he's called you to do.

Day 2
Exodus 12:21-27

Because of Pharaoh's stubbornness before God, God brought a series of plagues on the land of Egypt. He turned the Nile River to blood. He covered the people with boils. He sent hail. Plague after plague fell upon Egypt, but Pharaoh refused to let the Hebrews go.

The final plague was the death of all the firstborn children in Egypt. God told Moses the Hebrew children would be saved if blood from a lamb was placed on the doorframes of their homes. God gave specific instructions about how this was to be done. God was teaching his people to obey him.

There should always be a sharp contrast between the people who are stubborn and refuse to obey God and the people who belong to God and are quick to obey him. God's specific instructions for life can be found in his Word—the Bible.

When you know God's will about something, do you respond as Pharaoh did or are you quick to obey?

Even the Hebrews weren't very good at obeying God. Why do people find it so hard to obey God?

Day 3
Exodus 19:1-6

Moses had the awesome responsibility of speaking for God. What he told the people thousands of years ago still holds true today: Obey God and in return you'll receive the privilege of being called his own treasured possession. In the Old Testament, God called the Israelites his treasured possession. God now calls you his treasured possession if you've come to know him through Jesus Christ.

Take a minute to think about how incredible it is that the God of the universe wants to call you one of his treasured possessions. How do you feel about that?

What does it mean for you to be a treasured possession of God?

Ask God to help you live a life of obedience so he'll be pleased to refer to you as one of his treasured possessions.

Day 4
James 3:1-8

You've had many opportunities to hear people teach or preach about God. Speaking on behalf of God is a great honor and a huge responsibility. Perhaps Moses understood what a huge responsibility it is to speak for God and that's why he was reluctant to speak to Pharaoh.

If you've ever had a leadership role, such as teaching a class or leading a devotion, then you certainly know what an awesome responsibility it is to speak on behalf of God. As a result of this authority, God will judge teachers and preachers with greater strictness.

Do you feel God may be calling you to serve in some role of spiritual leadership?

Have you considered the demands and responsibilities placed on those who accept positions of leadership in God's kingdom?

Ask God to help you choose your words carefully and prayerfully when you speak for him.

Day 5
Exodus 24:3-8

The story of Moses begins with a hesitant man leading a reluctant group of people. But as the book of Exodus comes to a close, a confident Moses leads an obedient Hebrew nation. One of the great things about God's power is his ability to change people. One of the true marks of obeying God is the change that takes place in a person's life.

Since you started following God, how have you changed—

- *Spiritually?*
- *Socially?*
- *Emotionally?*
- *In other ways?*

Thank him for the positive changes he's made in your life.

WEEK 19
CALEB: FIRM CONVICTIONS

MEMORY VERSE

"But because my servant Caleb has a different spirit and follows me wholeheartedly, I will bring him into the land he went to, and his descendants will inherit it." (Numbers 14:24)

INTRODUCTION

The Hebrew people had escaped the slavery of Egypt and were preparing to enter the land promised to their ancestor Abraham. Because the land was inhabited, 12 spies were sent to check out the situation and bring a report back to Moses. Ten of the spies returned terrified of what they'd seen. They reported that the land was beautiful but that the enemies living there were too great to defeat. Two of the spies, Caleb and Joshua, agreed the land was magnificent and that the enemies were formidable; but they added that God would bring victory to his people.

Caleb and Joshua tried to reassure the Israelites, but the report of the 10 negative spies carried more weight in the eyes of the people. The tide of public opinion had turned, and God's people were paralyzed with fear. Caleb and Joshua weren't respected for standing up for their faith and convictions.

Most likely, you know how Caleb and Joshua felt.

Having firm convictions today sometimes means being in the minority. Someone said if you're a Christian and follow the crowd, then you're going in the wrong direction. Jesus said, "Small is the gate and narrow the road that leads to life, and only a few find it" (Matthew 7:14). Standing for God may mean standing apart from the rest of the crowd—as Caleb and Joshua did.

You may stand out, but you'll never stand alone. Caleb and Joshua found peace in knowing God would be with them always. And just as God continued to use Caleb and Joshua, he'll continue to use you.

DAILY DEVOTIONS

Day 1
Numbers 13:25-33

After the 40-day spy mission was complete, you can imagine the conversations among the 10 negative scouts. The exciting possibility of the Israelites inhabiting the Promised Land was replaced by the fear of giants. The fear of the 10 spies soon led to negativity, and that negative attitude undoubtedly grew by leaps and bounds.

Doubt and fear can quickly lead to discouragement when you face giants. You've probably seen that happen in your youth group. Maybe your group starts some new ministry, believing God will use it. Then some giant appears—financial problems, opposition from others in the church, difficulty with the needed materials—and people start giving up hope.

What are some giants you've faced or are facing in your life?

How do you approach these giants?

How can a Christian stay strong when facing a giant?

Ask God to help you to look up to him whenever you face overwhelming situations.

Day 2
Psalm 56:1-4

When the Israelites heard the negative reports about the land promised to them, the Bible tells us they were paralyzed with fear. The emotion of fear will keep you from having the courage to trust and obey God.

King David knew about fear. When he was younger, King Saul tried to kill him. David discovered that the best remedy for fear was to simply put his complete trust in God.

Do you fear anything right now? If so, what is it?

How completely are you trusting God? What do you need to trust him with?

Day 3
Numbers 14:26-35

Do you believe disobedience is a big deal to God? If you don't think a little disobedience is that big a deal, then consider the consequence the Israelites suffered for not obeying him: 40 years of wandering in the wilderness. To make things worse, God told them they'd learn what it was like to have Jehovah God as an enemy.

God is a God of grace and forgiveness, but he takes disobedience very seriously. You'll find peace, joy, and fulfillment as you obey God and follow him. When you live in direct disobedience to God, life can be very difficult.

Are you being disobedient in some area of your life right now?

Write a prayer in this journal. First, ask God to show you any areas of your life in which you're being disobedient to him. Next, repent of it. Finally, ask for God's help in being obedient to him.

Day 4
Matthew 7:13-23

Some people have estimated that only about 25 percent of the people in the world believe in Jesus. Of those who are Christians, only around 30 percent are growing in their faith and are passionate about what they believe. Jesus was right on target when he said very few people would ever find that narrow road.

Are you active in your youth group, walking daily with God, and passionate about your faith? If so, congratulations! That's a road very few people travel.

If you aren't among the 30 percent of Christians who're passionate about what they believe, and are growing in their faith—why not?

What do you need to change? Talking about it with God is a good place to start. You can never become the kind of Christian you want to be on your own; however, Jesus living in you can do it.

Day 5
Numbers 14:20-25

While the children of Israel learned there was a price for disobedience, Caleb discovered there was a reward for obeying God. His life was spared, he was allowed to enter the Promised Land, and his family had a full share of the new land. Our obedience to God may or may not be rewarded in this life, but we're promised a full share of a new land one day. You may have heard of this new land—it's called heaven.

Many Christians look forward to only what they'll receive here on earth as a reward for their obedience. Are you willing to obey God—as best you know how—even if it brings no earthly rewards?

If you can answer "yes" to that question, and if you are sincere in your response, then you show signs of being very spiritually mature. Thank God for how he's blessed you.

If you cannot answer that question positively, ask God to show you how to be obedient.

WEEK 20
JOSHUA: EQUIPPED AND EXALTED

MEMORY VERSE

"Do not let this Book of the Law depart from your mouth; meditate on it day and night, so that you may be careful to do everything written in it. Then you will be prosperous and successful." (Joshua 1:8)

INTRODUCTION

Imagine being a bricklayer one day and then the commander of an entire army the next. That's pretty much what happened to Joshua. Joshua served as Moses' assistant and simply did whatever he was asked to do. When Moses told Joshua to lead the people into the Promised Land, Joshua accepted his new role the only way he knew how—with a humble spirit and willing heart.

Joshua would go on to be a fearless leader in the battle for the land of Canaan. His relationship with Moses was a big help because he saw firsthand the mighty work God did through Moses. That gave Joshua confidence to move forward in the conquest.

Joshua's most important relationship was with God, because that was the true source of his strength. God promised Joshua victory. God promised he'd never fail or abandon Joshua. With the staff of Moses in his hand and the promises of God in his heart, Joshua became Israel's fearless leader.

In our society, people seem to believe the way to the top is to push and shove everyone out of the way. Today a great leader is viewed as someone who is feared, but Joshua became a great leader by being a great servant.

During Jesus' ministry he said if a person wanted to be great in God's kingdom, then that individual had to first learn to serve. This spiritual example of leadership still applies today because godly leaders always have humble, servantlike hearts. If you want to lead, then learn to serve.

DAILY DEVOTIONS

Day 1
Deuteronomy 31:1-8

Think about all the leaders in your church—teachers, staff members, deacons, the pastor. Just think: They were once students just as you are right now. And just as the role of leadership was passed to them, one day it'll be passed to you. God prepared Joshua to become the next leader of the Israelites after Moses, and God is preparing you to be part of the next generation of leaders in his kingdom. Are you ready?

How do you envision your leadership role in the church?

What do you see yourself doing to make a difference?

Ask God this week to help you be his kind of leader—not just in the future, but right now.

Day 2
Joshua 1:1-5

The first step in Joshua's life as a leader was learning his strength didn't come from himself; his source of strength was God. He'd seen the great things God did through Moses, and God promised Joshua he'd do the same kinds of things through him.

Have you ever stopped to think that the God who parted the Red Sea is the same God who lives in you? Great things are in store for you as well. Just remember, God is your source of strength as a leader.

What great things have you seen God do?

What expectations do you have for what God will do through you?

Ask God to use you just as he did Moses and Joshua.

Day 3
Joshua 1:6-18

Go back to today's passage and count the number of times God told Joshua to "be strong and courageous" in this one passage. Those words must have had special meaning for Joshua. He was about to lead the people into the Promised Land—the very land his people had fearfully resisted entering 40 years earlier.

Joshua knew the battle was God's, and that God would go before the Hebrews and fight for them. But it would still take courage and strength for Joshua to lead the people into a situation they feared.

Following God requires courage and strength. It may not seem too scary to show up at your church on a Sunday morning, but showing up is only a starting place. If you truly follow God, he'll take you where you cannot yet imagine. If you're serious about following God, then start working on your spiritual strength and courage. You'll need it.

What did God mean when he told Joshua to "be strong and courageous"?

How would you rate your own strength and courage?

Day 4
Mark 10:35-45

James and John were looking for greatness in Christ's kingdom. They wanted to be seated in the places of highest honor: On the right and left of Jesus. But Jesus told the disciples his kingdom was different: Leaders will be servants.

In heaven, places of honor aren't the thrones at the front of the room. Instead, the places of honor are at the back of the room, and they usually involve a mop or a broom. Greatness in the kingdom of God isn't measured by how well we're served but by how well we serve others.

Which is more important to you—to serve or to be served? Why?

If you don't desire to serve others, what things in your life need to change for you to become the kind of person Jesus wants you to be?

Pray for God to show you how to be great (by being a servant to others) each day.

Day 5
Psalm 1:1-6

As a leader Joshua learned God was his source of strength. God told Joshua to meditate on his Word day and night. The person who wrote the first psalm painted a great picture of that command. A tree planted by a river will never run out of water; it will also grow strong and vibrant.

The Bible is your river. If you stay in that river, your life will be nourished. You'll grow into a strong and vibrant follower of Christ.

Can you imagine a promise like that?

If you stay in God's Word, you'll grow into the person God wants you to be.

Are you planted by a stream of water—or are you planted in a parched desert?

Ask God to give you the desire to plant your life in his Word. Decide on a time to read his Word every day, and then ask God to help you be faithful.

WEEK 21
RAHAB: RISK AND GRACE

MEMORY VERSE

"By faith the prostitute Rahab, because she welcomed the spies, was not killed with those who were disobedient." (Hebrews 11:31)

INTRODUCTION

Joshua was preparing his plan of attack in the land of Canaan. He decided to send two spies to look over the site where the first battle would take place. Joshua was especially interested in checking out the fortress city of Jericho. While in the city, the spies' cover was blown, and they were saved by the most unlikely of heroes—a prostitute named Rahab.

Many biblical scholars have speculated about the woman named Rahab. The most interesting discussion centers on the scarlet cord that eventually saved her life and the lives of her family. Some scholars believe the scarlet cord was used in Old Testament times to designate the house of a prostitute. But when she saved the spies from the king of Jericho, they promised Rahab her family would be saved when the Hebrew soldiers took control of the city. And the distinguishing mark used to signal her salvation was the scarlet cord that hung in front of her house. Just think: The very thing that marked her immorality would become the instrument of her salvation.

God can redeem anyone in any situation. A life of immorality can be instantly changed by a demonstration of faith. Rahab's confession of her belief in God saved her physically—and eternally.

DAILY DEVOTIONS

Day 1
Joshua 2:1-7

The king of Jericho knew exactly what the spies were up to, but Rahab spared their lives by lying about their whereabouts. If the king had found out she was lying, Rahab surely would have been put to death. She put everything—even her life—on the line for her belief in God.

If you're like me, this story raises lots of questions. How did a prostitute come to have faith in the Hebrew God? How did these spies decide to hide in the home of a prostitute? Does this passage mean it was okay for her to lie to the king? Those are all good questions, but don't miss the point. Somehow Rahab put her trust in God. Somehow she knew to keep the spies safe. And God honored her faith in him.

When you bring a non-Christian friend to church, she may not know how people act at your church, including when to sit and when to stand. She might not dress like the people in your church. She might even use language that would singe the robes of your choir. But if she puts her faith in God, then everything will be forgiven.

Which of your friends have bad reputations—deserved or undeserved?

Have you given those friends a chance to know Jesus?

Day 2
Joshua 2:8-13

Rahab had heard the stories about the parting of the Red Sea. She'd heard about the Hebrews' conquests in other places. She believed God would give Jericho to the Hebrews as well.

Did you notice how Rahab described God?

Go back and read verse 11 again. That was quite an insight from not just a nonbeliever, but a nonbeliever of the most disrespected kind—a prostitute.

When you hear stories of things God has done, how do you respond?

Do stories of God's works inspire your faith?

Thank God you serve the Supreme Ruler of both heaven and earth.

Day 3
Joshua 2:14-21

The spies promised protection to all those who stayed inside Rahab's house when the Israelites took over the city of Jericho. Her house became a safe house for her family—and possibly others—when the fighting started. But as the spies had clearly pointed out, anyone who left Rahab's house wouldn't be safe. They'd face the same destruction as others in the city.

Our walk with God is much like that. When we're doing what he's called us to do, we're in his safe house. He takes care of us. But when we go outside God's protection by engaging in sin, we put ourselves in harm's way.

In what ways do you see God's protective hand in your life?

Can you think of a recent time when you felt that protection?

In what ways can you imagine a Christian stepping out of God's protective care?

What might be the result?

Day 4
Psalm 18:1-22

David was being pursued by King Saul. Saul was jealous of David and wanted him dead. When David wrote today's psalm, God had saved David from his enemies and from King Saul. David's sense of relief led to the writing of this beautiful passage.

Each day you face a world that has little regard for God. But if you live for God and truly seek to please him above all else, he'll be your Rock, your Fortress, and your Shield. He's your Protector.

Go to God today and thank him for the times he's been your Rock (to build life upon), your Fortress (to take refuge in), and your Shield (to keep you safe from the evil the world throws at you). Write some of your thoughts in this journal.

Day 5
Psalm 91:1-16

Have you ever thought about how keeping a promise protects you—and others? A parent's promise to stay married to a spouse protects the family from experiencing the terrible pain of divorce. When you keep your promises to your parents, you put their minds at ease. They're able to relax and trust you.

While promises made by people are sometimes broken, God's promises are not. They're 100 percent dependable. Make a habit of marking the promises of God in your Bible and praying these promises to God as your Protector.

What are some of God's promises to you in his Word?

What promise of God has meant the most to you?

Write a prayer of thanksgiving to God for these promises. Try to live in constant awareness of God's protection and provision.

WEEK 22
JOSHUA: THE FALL OF JERICHO

MEMORY VERSE

"By faith the walls of Jericho fell, after the people had marched around them for seven days." (Hebrews 11:30)

INTRODUCTION

The Promised Land consisted of groups of small city-states; each was governed and ruled by a separate king. As the Hebrews prepared to take the land, they had to fight not just one army but many armies.

The first battle took place at the city of Jericho, a city fortified by huge walls and gates. The prostitute Rahab hid the two Hebrew spies who sneaked into the city before the attack. Rather than scaling the walls of the city or attacking the doors with battering rams, God told his people to march around the city walls. So once a day for six days and then seven times on the seventh day the Hebrew soldiers marched around Jericho. No doubt that sounded like a strange military plan to the Israelites. But Joshua had learned the importance of trusting God and obeying him without question. He led the people to follow God's instructions to the letter.

Once the walls came down and Jericho was conquered, the battle moved to the city of Ai. Here the Israelites were soundly defeated. Why? This setback was due to the disobedience of just one person. God was continuing to teach his people how to obey him completely. After a time of repentance, a second confrontation with the people of Ai ended in victory for the Israelites.

Joshua lived the rest of his life as leader of the Israelites. When he passed away at the age of 110, there was a void in the leadership of Israel. The people had learned to trust God through Joshua, but now they were going to have to learn to trust God—period. The era of the judges was about to begin, and some very dark days were ahead for the children of Israel.

DAILY DEVOTIONS

Day 1
Joshua 6:1-7

Can you imagine Joshua saying something like, "Let's see if I have this right, God. We'll overtake a major city by marching around the walls, blowing trumpets, and shouting. Are you serious?" The Bible never suggests Joshua did anything but trust God. What God told him to do, he did. And it worked.

If we obey God only when it makes sense to us, then we'll never learn to really trust him. God has told you to forgive your enemies, to turn the other cheek when someone hits you, to love people who are trying to hurt you. Does that make sense? If not, then why should we do it? Because God said so. Is that enough of an answer for you? It was for Joshua.

Pray this week that you'll obey God—even when it doesn't seem logical.

Day 2
Joshua 7:1-9

The Hebrews had grown accustomed to winning battles. Perhaps they were learning to trust God, or perhaps they were beginning to believe they were self-sufficient. The army of Ai didn't seem to be much of a threat. Joshua sent a small army of about 3,000 men to take Ai, but Ai didn't fall. Rather, the army was beaten and a number of Israelite men were killed.

Some people turn to God only when they have big problems. Other people believe they can handle their own battles. They might never admit it, but they come to discount their need for God. Others take God for granted. They trust him to do what he's always done for them, but they don't approach God with humility and gratitude.

Do any of these descriptions fit you?

We cannot trust God with one battle in our lives and then be unfaithful in other areas. That was the problem the Hebrews experienced.

What battles are you entrusting to God? What battles do you need to entrust to God?

How are you responding to the ways God is working in your problems?

Pray that you'll be found faithful doing things with God, not just for him.

Day 3
Joshua 7:19-26

The Hebrew army was defeated because of the disobedience of one man: Achan. He took a robe, some silver coins, and a bar of gold from Jericho; but God had commanded them to leave alone these "devoted things" (Joshua 7:11). You may believe a little sin isn't as bad as a big one. But God expects and deserves total commitment and complete obedience.

On a scale of 1 to 10, how would you rate your total obedience to God in doing the things you know you're supposed to be doing?

Do you have a desire to be totally obedient?

If so, go to God and ask him to give you the strength, wisdom, and knowledge to be able to do so.

Day 4
Hebrews 11:23-31

The faith of Joshua was recorded and remembered thousands of years later—right next to the story of the life of Moses in the book of Hebrews. Did you notice that Joshua's act was recorded—but not his name? Of course, Joshua's name is remembered; it's just not listed in this roll call of faith.

Many faithful followers of God from throughout history aren't remembered at all. Who you are and even what you do may one day be forgotten here on earth, but your heavenly Father will never forget. He loves you and awaits the day he can reward your faith and your obedience.

Have you ever done something really good—yet received no outward recognition for it? If so, what was it?

Even if the world doesn't reward you for your faith, God sees and he knows. Let your goal be to seek God, not the recognition of the world.

Day 5
Joshua 24:14-24

Before Joshua died he gave a stirring speech to the people and challenged them to serve only God. But despite Joshua's challenging words, history reveals that the Hebrew people didn't keep their promise to serve God. Instead, they repeatedly fell into the habit of worshiping false gods.

Joshua could speak only for himself and his family. You must make the same choice. You'll have to decide for yourself if you will serve the Lord.

Will you commit to serving God—every day—for the rest of your life?

If so, write today's date in this journal and sign your name as your promise to serve and live for God from this point on.

Ask God to give you the strength to make—and keep—this commitment. But also realize that God will give you grace when you fall short of complete obedience to him.

WEEK 23
JUDGE GIDEON: AN UNLIKELY HERO

MEMORY VERSES

"'But Lord,' Gideon asked, 'how can I save Israel? My clan is the weakest in Manasseh, and I am the least in my family.' The Lord answered, 'I will be with you, and you will strike down all the Midianites together.'" (Judges 6:15-16)

INTRODUCTION

Two hundred years had passed since the victories of Joshua in the land of Canaan. Many changes had taken place—most of them weren't good. The Promised Land was occupied by many enemies, and the Israelites were spending much of their time hiding in fear. During this time of oppression, God called out leaders known as "judges," or deliverers to rescue his people.

This was the time of a man named Gideon. God called on him to deliver the Hebrew people from a group of nomadic fighters known as the Midianites. God saw a mighty warrior in Gideon. Gideon, however, saw himself as a weakling. He told God he was the weakest person from the weakest family in the weakest tribe in all of Israel. God showed Gideon—through a series of signs—that he'd be the one God would use. Gideon was finally convinced.

When it came time for the big fight with the Midianites, Gideon felt pretty good about his army of 32,000—until God whittled the number down to just 300 men. Then God led Gideon and his tiny army to victory, and the people were delivered from their enemy.

Gideon was an unlikely hero—an average person who didn't think very highly of himself. His life was changed when the God of the ages touched him with the power of encouragement. God saw Gideon's potential and understood he was a person who'd always know that his ability to lead was a gift from God.

DAILY DEVOTIONS

Day 1
Judges 6:11-13

The Israelites had been unfaithful to God. They had begun worshiping the idols of the people groups living around them. Because of their unfaithfulness, God allowed them to be attacked by outside enemies. The people cried out to God to save them.

When God called Gideon to fight and save his people, he demonstrated two things. The first was his great and constant love for his people. God still cared for Israel. Even though they'd failed him, God was about to make a way to save them. Second, God saw qualities in Gideon that Gideon hadn't seen in himself. Gideon saw himself as weak and insignificant. God saw him as a faithful leader who'd depend on the power of God rather than his own abilities.

God may show you great qualities you never realized you possessed. Since God made you, he knows you better than anyone—including yourself.

Pray this week that you'll begin to see yourself as God sees you. Don't ask God to show you things about yourself so you can feel proud. Rather, ask him to show you more about yourself so you can be more useful to him.

Day 2
Judges 6:14-21

How would you feel if an angel visited you? Several times this happened to various people in the Bible, including Gideon. But when an angel told Gideon he (Gideon) was a mighty warrior and that God was with him, his response was predictable: Gideon pointed out all his own inadequacies.

Most of us do the same thing. God has chosen us as Christians to do great things for him, but our response is usually focused on our weaknesses. "I could never speak in front of a group," "I could never witness to her," or "I could never..." (fill in the blank). Instead, the best response to God's call is to always say, "God, I'm ready."

Which do you have—a "can do" spirit or a "can't do" spirit?

Ask God to help you trust him to do the things he wants to do through you.

Day 3
Psalm 77:1-15

The writer of today's Scripture passage was depressed. He thought back to times of victory and joy, and he longed for those days. Gideon and his people were hiding out in fear of the Midianites. They must have had the same kinds of feelings.

At this point in your Christian life, are you living in the joy of the Lord and experiencing spiritual victory—or are you simply remembering those things as part of the good old days? Determine to live your life in such a way that great days with God are never a thing of the past.

Which is true for you right now: "My Christian life was so much better in the past," or "My Christian life is strong now"?

What are you doing—or not doing—to make it this way?

What do you need to change to be able to say, "My Christian life is strong now"?

Ask God to help you change. God will help you if you truly desire it.

Day 4
Judges 7:1-8

The odds seemed pretty good when Gideon started out with an army of 32,000. But when God reduced that number to 300, Gideon must have been more than just a little worried. Nevertheless, Gideon discovered that great things happen when the power of God is added to any situation.

Always remember that you plus God equals a majority. That's how God works. He can arrange—or rearrange—hopeless-looking situations and turn them into victories.

Have you ever faced a situation like Gideon's in which things seemed hopeless but came out well in the end? If so, what was it?

Ask God to help you see your own helplessness and trust totally in his worthiness.

Day 5
Judges 8:22-27

Gideon did a wonderful thing by pointing the people to God when they asked him to be their ruler. But later, when the Israelites started worshiping the golden ephod Gideon asked them to make, it was clear they just wanted to worship a physical object. This is a perfect example of getting caught up in the trap of putting all our attention on the things of God instead of focusing on God himself. This is never right, and it doesn't please God. In fact, it's idolatry.

What would it mean today if we were to worship the things of God instead of worshiping God?

Can you think of situations in which you've worshiped the things of God instead of God himself?

Take some time right now to focus entirely on God and who he is to you. Ask him to help you worship him only, not the things associated with him.

WEEK 24
JUDGE SAMSON: A POWERFUL DEATH

MEMORY VERSE

"No one serving as a soldier gets involved in civilian affairs—he wants to please his commanding officer." (2 Timothy 2:4)

INTRODUCTION

Once again, God chose to deliver his people from their enemies. This time the action took place south of where Gideon lived, and the enemies were known as the Philistines.

One day an angel appeared to a couple from the tribe of Dan. He told them they'd have a long-awaited child—a son—and they should dedicate the child as a Nazirite. The angel also said their son would rescue Israel from the Philistines. This son the angel referred to was Samson.

Samson was an awesome physical specimen. He had the potential to be a great leader, but ego and self-centeredness would eventually bring down this mighty man of God. Early in his life, Samson insisted his father get him a Philistine woman to be his wife, even though her people worshiped the false god Dagon. Later, Samson's lust for Delilah blinded him to her efforts to discover and ultimately remove the secret to his strength—his long hair.

Samson, the great and powerful man of God, lived his final days blind and in captivity, like an animal. The Philistines mocked his former strength by chaining him to a device used to grind wheat in a mill. But with his hair growing back and his strength slowly returning, Samson prayed that God would allow him to take revenge on those who blinded him. God granted his request, and Samson pulled down the pillars of the temple, killing more Philistines that day than he'd done over the course of his lifetime.

Samson's physical power was great, but he wasn't a great person. He went out with a bang, but a consecrated lifetime spent following God would have made a greater impact on history. Samson's life was unrealized potential that produced a whole lot of fizzle.

As a follower of God, are you realizing the potential God has given you?

DAILY DEVOTIONS

Day 1
Judges 13:1-7

The Nazirite vow was a special commitment to God. Numbers 6:1-21 describes the vow in detail. Take a minute to scan that passage now.

You probably noticed that a Nazirite vow was taken for a specific amount of time. At the end of the time period, the person who made the vow would make a sacrifice and shave his head. God's command for Samson, however, was that he should remain a Nazirite for life— and that was very unusual.

The Nazirite vow required a person not to drink grape juice or wine, cut his hair, or touch any dead body. When God told Samson's mother she wasn't to drink wine while she was pregnant, it indicated even before he was born that Samson wouldn't touch wine. Samson was to be completely set apart for God's use.
You'd be unusual if you took a Nazirite vow. However, God's desire for your life is that you be set apart for his service. God desires that your life be free of anything that would distract you from fully following him.

Is there anything in your life that distracts you from God's service?

If so, what should you do about it?

Day 2
Judges 14:1-20

Samson's courtship with the pagan Philistine woman was a disaster. Samson wound up killing 30 men and then going home to his mom and dad while his bride-to-be married the best man. Samson is a great example of how feelings for someone of the opposite sex can lead you into choices that can disrupt your life.

As you choose people to date, you should choose people who will enhance your walk with God. If you date someone who distracts you from your walk with God, it could lead to dry times in your life, difficulties at home, and missed opportunities in ministry. It's even possible it could lead to a complete disaster, just as Samson's relationship did.

What standards do you have for the people you date?

You may not be dating at this point in your life. But, to be honest, choosing the kind of people you'll date before you start dating is a real help.

Day 3
Psalm 146:1-10

Not long ago I was fortunate enough to vacation at beautiful Lake Tahoe. The lake is 1,600 feet deep, the second deepest lake in America. It's approximately 4,500 feet above sea level. The water is so still, clear, and calm in Lake Tahoe that it's said one can see a hundred feet into its depths.

For me Lake Tahoe is an incredible picture of the peace Christians can feel. Turmoil may surround them, but they can still feel a deep tranquility that comes only from God.

Do you have peace or turmoil in your life?

What's the reason for this?

Day 4
Judges 16:4-17

Maybe Samson wasn't the brightest guy around, or maybe he just caved to the relentless whining of a beautiful woman. But whatever the case, he gave up the secret of his strength.

Samson was born for a great purpose, but he allowed himself to be manipulated into giving up what was most important. Samson was foolish enough to compromise his character and strength for a woman who was clearly using him.

What leads you to compromise in your life?

Is there anything that causes you to compromise your character?

Would you compromise your character by cheating in order to get a good grade?

Would you compromise your relationship with your parents by lying to them so you could do something they'd otherwise tell you not to do?

Make some notes in the journal about the areas of your life that are easy for you to compromise. Ask God to help you stay strong in your faith so you can overcome the temptations that could pull you away from him.

Day 5
Judges 16:21-30

One statement in today's passage sticks out above the rest for me. It's the last part of the last verse: Samson killed more Philistines by dying than he did by living. In other words, he accomplished more for God by dying than he ever did by living. Even though he managed to kill many of the evil Philistines while committing suicide, he wasted most of his life. While "going out with a bang" may sound like a great way to go, the way we live our entire lives is the true test of a life lived for God.

In what ways is your life counting for God?

In what ways could your life count more for God?

Stay in tune with God day by day. That's the way to make sure your life will count.

WEEK 25
RUTH: REDEMPTION AND BLESSINGS

MEMORY VERSES

"Do nothing out of selfish ambition or vain conceit, but in humility consider others better than yourselves. Each of you should look not only to your own interests, but also to the interests of others." (Philippians 2:3-4)

INTRODUCTION

It seems as though all the Bible characters we've studied over the past few months have been defined by either their obedience to God or their disobedience to him.

The story of Ruth helps us look at the role of obedience in the lives of God's people. In it we see how obedience leads to her redemption as well as the redemption of all humanity—including you.

Things were different for women in Ruth's day. When her husband died unexpectedly, Ruth was left with no security and no way to earn a living. Her mother-in-law, Naomi, encouraged Ruth to stay in Moab with her own people. But Ruth's faithfulness to Naomi—whose husband had also died—led both women to journey to Israel. Ruth provided food for herself and for her mother-in-law by picking up bits of grain during harvest time in the barley fields. Then a man named Boaz—the man who owned the field—spotted her.

What was it about Ruth that caught the eye of Boaz? Could it have been her outward beauty? Her godly character? When Boaz asked about Ruth, people told him she'd returned to the land with her mother-in-law, Naomi. The foreman over the field workers told Boaz about Ruth's hard work in the field. Her character must have appealed to Boaz because he immediately went to talk with her, and he tried to help her as much as possible.

When Boaz married Ruth, he saved her from a life of hardship. God's plan of redemption was also at work in the lives of Ruth and Boaz. Their son Obed was King David's grandfather—an ancestor to Jesus Christ, the Redeemer of the world.

DAILY DEVOTIONS

Day 1
Ruth 1:6-18

You may have attended a wedding during which verses 16 and 17 were quoted as words of commitment between the husband and wife. Those words are poetic and express marriage commitment well, but they weren't originally spoken between spouses. This was a commitment Ruth made to her mother-in-law. The words reveal the loving and selfless nature of Ruth's heart.

Real love is not self-serving. Whether between a husband and a wife, a parent and a child, or two good friends, real love is about a commitment to God's very best for the other person. Obviously, you cannot move every time a close friend moves away, but you can continue your commitment to your friendship through e-mails, letters, phone calls, and visits. And when a friend does something to hurt you, your commitment should lead you to be quick to forgive.

Do you exhibit true, honest, and godly love toward others, or is your love based on selfishness and what they can do for you?

Pray this week that you'll exhibit real, godly love.

Day 2
Ruth 2:1-7

Boaz was a godly man. Notice how he greeted the workers harvesting his field by saying, "The Lord be with you!" Boaz showed himself to be a man who loved God and a man of good character. His love for Ruth grew out of his commitment to God. He saw something unique in her commitment to her mother-in-law. One of the most—if not the most—beautiful love stories in the Bible is the story of Ruth and Boaz.

What do you value in people of the opposite sex? Outward beauty is nice. You may like a person's sense of humor or personality. Those attributes are good. However, if you want your relationships to be godly, then you have to look a little deeper. When you choose someone to date, don't be in a hurry. Look for someone with a deep love for God and a strong, godly character.

If you're in a dating relationship now, think about why you're dating that girl or guy. What attracts you to that person?

What godly attributes do you see in his or her life?

Pray that God would give you eyes to see what he desires in a person of the opposite sex.

Day 3
Ruth 2:8-16

The people at your school probably won't congratulate you on your good character, but you can be sure they're watching you. Boaz saw and appreciated the sacrifices Ruth made even though she probably had no idea he was watching her. Living the Christian life day by day is one way we share Christ with others. Don't be discouraged; keep striving to live a godly life. Someone is being affected by the way you're living your life today.

If others are closely watching your character, what do they see?

Are there ways you need to improve your character? If so, how?

Ask God to help you be consistent in living for him.

Day 4
Ruth 3:1-9

Ruth went right on showing respect for Naomi by following her and obeying her instructions. Even though she was a grown woman who'd been married once herself and even though she had no obligation to obey her mother-in-law, she did—and was wise for doing so. Obeying your parents is an excellent way to show respect for them. In Exodus 20:12 we find this command and promise, "Honor your father and your mother, so that you may live long in the land the Lord your God is giving you."

Your obedience to your parents shows a lot about your character. If you fail to honor your parents, then you probably won't honor God in your other relationships. But if you honor your parents, then you'll probably be the kind of person who sticks with friends in hard times.

How is your attitude toward your parents?

Are there any changes you need to make?

Day 5
Psalm 15

The story of Ruth shows the importance of godly character. It also reveals the benefits of godly character. Ruth and Boaz found deep love for each other. Ruth was honored, and she even became one of the ancestors of Jesus Christ.

Psalm 15 includes a list of some godly characteristics. As you journal write down all the characteristics you can find in that passage.

How well do these characteristics describe you?

Ask God to develop these characteristics in your life.

WEEK 26
HANNAH: PLEA AND PRAISE

MEMORY VERSES

"'I prayed for this child, and the Lord has granted me what I asked of him. So now I give him to the Lord. For his whole life he will be given over to the Lord.' And he worshiped the Lord there." (1 Samuel 1:27-28)

INTRODUCTION

Many churches hold baby dedication services once or twice a year. Parents stand with their babies at the front of the church and make a promise to both God and the congregation that their child will learn Christian beliefs and values. How would you react if, at the end of the service, a mother gave her son to the pastor and said that since she'd prayed for a child and her prayer was answered, she wanted to give him up to serve God? That's similar to what a woman in the Old Testament did with her son.

Elkanah had two wives, Peninnah and Hannah. Peninnah had children, but Hannah did not. Childless Hebrew women were viewed as dishonored by God. And to add to Hannah's anguish, Peninnah made fun of her constantly for not having any children. During her yearly visit to the temple, Hannah poured out her soul to God in prayer. She made a vow that if God would give her a son, she'd dedicate him totally to God.

God answered Hannah's prayer for a son quickly and completely. She became pregnant and had Samuel, which means "heard of the Lord." Hannah also kept her promise. After Samuel was weaned, she brought him to the priest, Eli, for service to God. She literally gave her son to God.

Sometimes you may believe God isn't answering your prayers. But regardless of how you feel, the God of the universe will always hear your prayer. And God answers every prayer in his time and in his way.

DAILY DEVOTIONS

Day 1
1 Samuel 1:9-18

Hannah was in anguish over her inability to have children. Her prayer was a time of "pouring out her soul to God." In fact, she was so absorbed in her prayer that the priest actually thought she was drunk.

Are your prayers like standard form letters or do you reveal your soul to God? Even though God knows your mind and your heart, he wants you to share your inmost thoughts, goals, dreams, desires, and fears with him.

How deeply do you pray?

Beginning today, adopt the attitude of Hannah as you pray. Don't settle for ordinary praying. Try pouring out your heart before God.

Day 2
1 Samuel 1:19-28

Hannah did just what she promised: She gave up her only son for God's service. When Samuel was able to take solid food, she took him to the priest at the temple and left him there to be raised in God's service. Samuel was her only child—a child she'd begged God for—and she gave him up. She made a costly commitment, and she kept it.

Over the years I've heard many students make prayer promises to God. Some (probably many; maybe even most) of those promises were never kept.

You may tell God you'll do things for him when you're desperate for him to answer a prayer. But how often are you really sincere when it comes to making a commitment to God?

Are you serious enough about your commitments to God to follow through as Hannah did?

Is there a commitment you need to make to God? What is it?

What would it take for you to live out this commitment?

Day 3
1 Samuel 2:1-10

Is there any greater joy than when God answers your prayer quickly and completely? God delights in giving his children gifts just as most earthly fathers do. He'll not give us everything we ask for because we often ask for the wrong things. But he hears our prayers and gives us what will bring him honor.

When God answered Hannah's prayer for a child, she was so filled with awe that she prayed a beautiful song to God found in today's reading. Her joy poured out in love to God as she acknowledged all his goodness and mercy. She sang of his limitless strength. Hannah's heart overflowed with thanksgiving for God's gift.

It's really easy to pray for something you want or need; it's a lot harder to stop and remember to thank God when he answers your prayer. A good rule is to spend as much time and effort thanking God after he answers your prayer as you spend asking for the prayer to be answered.

Are you really thankful when God answers a prayer you know only God could answer?

How do you express your thanks to God?

Day 4
Psalm 4:1-8

"Can you hear me now?" If you own a cell phone, you probably hear that phrase a lot. If you're in certain locations—inside or outside—the reception isn't always great with cell phones.

You never have to ask God whether he can hear you. The God of the universe never sleeps. He's always on call. He doesn't need antennas, satellites, or a good location outside or next to the window to hear you better. Every time you pray, you can be sure you're getting through to God—loud and clear.

How does it make you feel to know God can hear you perfectly anytime, anyplace?

Why don't you talk to him now—knowing he hears you at this very moment loud and clear?

Day 5
Psalm 116:1-19

It's an awesome experience to realize the God of the universe has heard you and given you the desire of your heart. The person who wrote today's psalm experienced the joy of answered prayer. I love the mental picture of God bending down like an adult to a child and listening to our prayer requests. The psalmist responds to the goodness of God by promising to pray as long as he has breath.

What prayers have you seen answered recently?

Not every time of prayer will be filled with the wonder and joy expressed in this psalm. However, times of wonder and joy are special times with God. How are your times of prayer with God? Are they full of wonder and joy?

How could you deepen your times with God?

WEEK 27
SAMUEL: HEARING GOD'S VOICE

MEMORY VERSE

"The Lord continued to appear at Shiloh, and there he revealed himself to Samuel through his word." (1 Samuel 3:21)

INTRODUCTION

It's always been tough to be a godly young person, even in Old Testament days. Consider the life of young Samuel. He was raised in the temple by the high priest Eli and had to live around Eli's sons, Hophni and Phinehas, who were also priests. To say these two sons were bad news is an understatement. They'd keep the best part of meat sacrifices for themselves, they seduced young women at the temple, and they had no respect for God. But even though Samuel was surrounded by bad influences, he continued to do things that were pleasing to God.

When Samuel was very young, he heard the voice of God one night. The Bible states that visions and messages from God were rare in those days. And as Samuel grew, so did his reputation as a godly man and a man of wisdom. God continued to speak to Samuel and used him to prepare Israel for the transition from the period of the judges to the period of the kings.

One of the wisest man who ever lived, Solomon, wrote in Ecclesiastes 12:1, "Remember your Creator in the days of your youth, before the days of trouble come and the years approach when you will say, 'I find no pleasure in them.'" John Wesley said Solomon's negative reference to old age was due to his looking back with regret over his teenage years.

Can God do great things in the life of a teenager? He certainly did with Samuel.

Is it possible for a teenager to resist negative peer pressure and live a life that pleases God? Samuel did that very thing his entire life.

Are you living your life in a way that honors God? Will you be able to one day look back over your teenage years with no regrets?

DAILY DEVOTIONS

Day 1
1 Samuel 2:18-21

You may have heard it said, "You can't out-give God." No matter what you may believe you're sacrificing to God, he'll give you more from his abundant riches (which are endless). Of course, that doesn't mean that if you put a few bucks in the offering plate, then God will give you a hot sports car. But it does mean that when you entrust your life and resources to God unselfishly, he'll fill your life with meaning, love, and hope.

Hannah experienced the incredible blessings of God firsthand. After she gave her only son, Samuel, to God's service, God blessed her with five more children. Hannah's blessings were the result of her ability to put her total confidence in God.

Honestly, do you really trust God—or is it just something you say that sounds spiritual? Why or why not?

What sacrifices have you made to God?

How has he blessed you in return for your service? Make some notes as you journal.

Pray this week that you'll begin letting go of the things keeping you from really trusting in God.

Day 2
1 Samuel 3:1-10

God spoke to Samuel in such a clear voice that Samuel thought another person was speaking. He reasoned Eli must be calling out to him during the night. The Bible says God rarely spoke to people in that day—perhaps because few people were listening. And despite the fact that Eli served in the temple, it still took him several times to realize who was speaking to Samuel. Finally, Eli began to suspect Samuel was hearing the very voice of God.

So how was Samuel supposed to figure out what God wanted to say to him? Eli told Samuel to say, "Speak, Lord, for your servant is listening." If you want to hear what God has to say, then you have to start listening for him.

Do you feel you're close enough to God that if he spoke your name, you'd know who it was? Why or why not?

Abide in God's presence today. The closer you are to him, the more clearly you'll hear his voice.

Day 3
1 Samuel 12:1-7

In today's passage Samuel is an old man. The people had been calling for a king so they could be like other nations. God warned them a king would bring more strife into their lives, but the people continued to beg for one. Finally, God sent Samuel to anoint Saul as their first king.

Afterward, as Samuel stood before the people, he recalled his life. Samuel was able to say he'd maintained high morals and a godly character. Despite the rebellion of the people in wanting a king, Samuel claimed he'd carefully followed the instructions of God. You may take pride in living that kind of life for a few days, weeks, or months; but Samuel lived that way his entire life. His secret was simply to trust and obey God every day.

What kind of priority is it for you to live a life pleasing to God?

Ask God to help you make living for him the priority in your life.

Day 4
Psalm 34:1-22

Did you notice the word taste in this passage? Read verse 8 again. Some commentaries on this passage use the words try and experience instead of the word taste.

The writer is challenging you to experience a life of trusting God. The result will be finding out that God is good and that joy will follow. While it can be scary to step out in faith and trust God, you'll be rewarded by experiencing God in a whole new way. You cannot grow unless you're stretched.

Can you think of a time you've tasted God's goodness?

What's it like?

Pray you'll be able to taste God's goodness today.

Day 5
Proverbs 3:1-8

It's so easy to depend on your own understanding. But when you do that, you obviously aren't trusting God. God's understanding is perfect, and he wants to guide you every moment of every day and in every situation.

So how do you come to understand God's understanding of things? Start by reading the Bible and letting his truth and wisdom permeate your mind.

Can you honestly say you trust in God?

If you said "yes," then what are some recent examples of your trust in him?

Pray today that you'll learn the true meaning of trusting in God—not in your own abilities or wisdom.

WEEK 28
KING SAUL: ISRAEL'S FIRST KING

MEMORY VERSE

"But now your kingdom will not endure; the Lord has sought out a man after his own heart and appointed him leader of his people, because you have not kept the Lord's command." (1 Samuel 13:14)

INTRODUCTION

In one episode of the television classic *The Andy Griffith Show*, Aunt Bea ran for city council. Her motto was that if the people of Mayberry wanted something, she'd do her best to accomplish it. Her opponent, Howard Sprague, pointed out that what people wanted wasn't necessarily what was best for them.

The period of the judges was coming to an end. Samuel, the last of the judges, was growing old. His sons were greedy and corrupt, not suitable successors. The people cried out for a king to lead them so they could be like other nations. Samuel told them a king would draft their sons for battle and make slaves of their daughters. He pointed out that a king would tax them and take their crops and cattle. Still the people cried for a king.

Saul became the first king of Israel at the age of 30, and he ruled for 42 years. A few victories in the early years of his reign convinced the Hebrews they'd made the right choice. Then things started going downhill. Saul showed impatience and a lack of respect for the priesthood by offering his own sacrifice. Then, during a battle with the Amalekites, Saul disobeyed Samuel's instructions by not killing King Agag. The book of 1 Samuel records that God was sorry he'd made Saul king of Israel.

The overall failure of Saul's rule as king can be summed up in one word—disobedience. The Hebrew people were disobedient to God when they demanded a king, and Saul was disobedient in many of his actions while he was king. But God's purposes always prevail, and the best days in the history of Israel were about to begin.

DAILY DEVOTIONS

Day 1
1 Samuel 8:1-9

Read God's answer to Samuel's prayer in verses 7-8 one more time. When the Israelites cried out for a king, they were rejecting God's leadership and protection. God had led the people of Israel out of Egypt. He'd given them the Promised Land. He'd raised up judges when the enemies of Israel attacked them. He'd been their good and benevolent King. Amazingly, the people of Israel wanted to rely on a weak, human king rather than the almighty God.

It's easy to see how wrong the Israelites were in rejecting God as their King. However, we may not be that different. When we let our culture or our friends dictate our values and character, we're rejecting God's leadership. Does God determine the language you use, or do your friends determine what words you say? Do you look to movies and television shows as patterns for your relationships with the opposite sex, or do you find godly patterns in God's Word?

Which do you strive for: What everyone else desires for you to do, or what God desires for you to do? Make some notes as you journal.

Pray this week that you'll have a renewed passion for relying on God for everything.

Day 2
1 Samuel 9:14-27

Saul felt very inadequate when Samuel told him the hope of Israel rested on his shoulders. Saul's problem was that he never realized he needed to rely on God instead of relying on himself.

If you believe God sometimes calls you to do things you can't handle, then you're right. God will give you things bigger than you are so you'll have to trust him.

You need to rely on God, not on your own strength, wisdom, or abilities. What you do when you're relying on God may be different than what makes sense to you—or to others. But God has you right where he wants you when that happens.

Think back on some of the spiritual decisions you've made recently. Did you trust yourself or did you lean on God?

Pray that you'll have the wisdom to trust God, not yourself.

Day 3
1 Samuel 13:5-14

When Saul offered his own sacrifice, his true nature was revealed. He was impatient; he didn't respect the office of the priesthood God had established; and he showed an inability to obey God.

Waiting on God can be hard work. Do you remember what Abraham did when it took God longer to give Sarah a child than Abraham thought it should? He took matters into his own hands and had a child with Sarah's handmaiden (Genesis 16). You may have some things in your life you want so badly you can taste them. Be careful. Don't get ahead of God. He'll bring you the best in his time.

Think: Is there anything in your life you're waiting for God to do? If so, what is it?

How difficult is it for you to wait for God's timing?

Day 4
Psalm 33:12-22

Have you ever gone so far out on a limb with God that your only possible chance of success was through his power? God wants us to stop relying on our wisdom, our strength, our abilities, and ourselves, and put our trust in him. Today's key verse contains this promise: "But the eyes of the Lord are on those who fear him, on those whose hope is in his unfailing love" (verse 18). That's some kind of bodyguard.

Which of your own strengths do you tend to rely on instead of relying on God? Looks? Smarts? Personality? Athletic ability?

Remember that your best strength is God himself. Pray to God that he'll show you how to rely on him daily.

Day 5
1 Samuel 15:10-19

I once had a student tell me that the worst punishment his parents could give him was saying they were disappointed in him. What do you think about that? How much pain would you personally feel if you knew God were disappointed in you? That would really hurt, wouldn't it?

God is a God of incredible grace and forgiveness. We've all failed him at times, yet he chooses to love us, forgive us, and clean us up to make us usable again. But never use God's forgiveness as a license to live a disappointing life. Make the choice to live today in a way that will be pleasing to your heavenly Father.

What word describes how you'd feel if you knew God were disappointed with how you lived or acted?

Tell God about your desire to please him and to be a blessing to him.

WEEK 29
DAVID AND JONATHAN: A DEEP FRIENDSHIP

MEMORY VERSE

"By this all men will know that you are my disciples, if you love one another."
(John 13:35)

INTRODUCTION

The story of David and Jonathan is a story of true friendship. David was commissioned to calm King Saul's spirit with the harp. When David met Jonathan, Saul's son, they became instant friends. That friendship would be tested many times as Saul's jealousy of David grew.

God was with David. His victories in battle made him a celebrity. King Saul became jealous and tried many times to kill David. Once Jonathan talked his father out of a murderous plan. Another time Jonathan helped David escape from his father. Jonathan put his own life on the line for his friend David.

Because he was the oldest son, Jonathan was the heir to the throne of Israel. Yet Jonathan recognized the anointing God had placed on David, and he told him that one day David would be the next king. Jonathan was perfectly content with the idea of serving alongside David as second in command. But his wish would never come true. Both Jonathan and Saul died during a battle with the Amalekites. David mourned and fasted over the death of his good friend.

If you want to have good friends, then you have to be a good friend. David and Jonathan were willing to die for each other. David summed up his love for his friend in a funeral song he wrote about Saul and Jonathan (see 2 Samuel 1:17-27).

Wouldn't you love to have a friend like that? Are you willing to be a friend like that?

DAILY DEVOTIONS

Day 1
1 Samuel 18:1-9

Most friendships develop over time. You probably have friends you've learned to appreciate as you've gotten to know them. But have you ever found a friend who became your closest friend the first time you ever met? That was the case with David and Jonathan. Their friendship and love for each other was instant.

Whether your bond with him is immediate or gradual, a good friend is truly a gift from God. True friends—like David and Jonathan—help each other, laugh when the other is happy, and cry when the other is sad. A true friend is priceless.

Pray for your friends by name today. Thank God for the special people he's placed in your life.

Day 2
1 Samuel 19:1-7

A good friend will always stand up for you and stick by your side. David and Jonathan's friendship was so strong that Jonathan spoke against his father's kingly command and urged his father not to kill David. As a result, Saul changed his mind. True friendship can overcome many things, and it can even right many wrongs.

Don't misunderstand the point. Close friendship doesn't mean betraying the trust of your parents. Jonathan's father was planning to murder David. Your parents may dislike your friends, but they probably don't have any homicidal plans for them. Don't make the mistake of being disloyal to your parents while you're trying to be loyal to your friends.

Would your friends describe you as loyal?

What does it mean to be loyal to a friend?

What circumstances have made it hard for you to stand by a friend in the past? How did you handle it?

How do you wish you'd handled it differently?

Pray that you'll be the kind of friend Jonathan was to David.

Day 3
1 Samuel 20:1-17

Here we see once again that David was running for his life from King Saul—and once again Jonathan was there to help his best friend. As their friendship grew deeper, David and Jonathan vowed to protect each other and to watch over each other's families; then they reaffirmed their friendship. Godly friends look out for each other. David and Jonathan had each other's backs.

Who has your back?

Whose back do you have?

Ask God to help you be the kind of friend who'll be willing to sacrifice something important, if necessary. Pray that you'll be such a good friend that others will be willing to do the same for you.

Day 4
Proverbs 27:1-6

A real friend will be honest with you. Wise King Solomon said, "Wounds from a sincere friend are better than many kisses from an enemy" (Proverbs 27:6, NLT). In other words, real friends can be honest with each other even if it hurts.

While some friends might get upset with you if you're honest with them, can you say these people are really your friends? This doesn't mean you should try to be rude to your friends just to see how they'll respond. It does mean you can share the truth with them—in a loving way—and they'll still love you.

Has your friendship with someone reached the point where you both feel comfortable being totally honest with each other?

When have you experienced wounds from a friend as something you really needed?

Pray that you'll develop friendships that are honest.

Day 5
John 15:9-17

The greatest measure of love is when someone lays down her life for a friend. Have you ever considered whether you'd ever give your life for someone else? A mother might give her life for a son. A husband might sacrifice his life for his wife. But a friend would have to mean a lot for you to sacrifice your life for him.

It's hard to even think about dying for someone else—even a true friend. But that's exactly what Jesus did for us. He died in our place. Now we have the honor of being called friends of God. What an awesome phrase to describe Christians—a phrase we really don't deserve.

Have you ever considered yourself a friend of God? Why or why not?

Ask God to help you discover the depth and richness of a friendship with him.

WEEK 30
KING DAVID: SEEKING GOD'S HEART

MEMORY VERSE

"After removing Saul, he made David their king. He testified concerning him: 'I have found David son of Jesse a man after my own heart; he will do everything I want him to do.'" (Acts 13:22)

INTRODUCTION

When David was young, he was a shepherd who looked after his father's sheep. He spent his days looking for grazing land, protecting the sheep from wild animals, and thinking. A shepherd's life is lonely, and David had a lot of time to think about God. As a musician, he took many of those thoughts and created some of the great passages in the book of Psalms. David had a heart for God.

During those years the Israelites were locked in a fierce battle with the Philistines. Their chief warrior was a giant known as Goliath. He stood nine feet tall and carried a spear with a tip that weighed 15 pounds. While David was delivering some food to his three brothers serving in the Israelite army, he heard the challenge from Goliath. David couldn't believe no one would fight this man who dared to defy the army of the living God.

With five smooth stones and a sling, David took on the giant. The years David spent in solitude as a shepherd prepared him for this battle. While he was experienced with a sling, a weapon he'd used to protect his sheep from wild animals, his greatest assets were a heart for God and a belief that with God anything was possible. Armed with courage and the Spirit of the Lord, David took down the giant with one stone.

The Bible states that David was a man after God's own heart. And his love for God had intensified during his lonely days as a shepherd boy.

So when it came time to stand up to a pagan giant, David quickly took the challenge because of his deep love for God.

David would soon become the king of Israel. God was preparing to use David in a powerful way.

DAILY DEVOTIONS

Day 1
1 Samuel 17:24-32

David was amazed the soldiers of Israel would allow a Philistine to defy God's army. How dare he mock God and his army! David was probably a young teenager; he definitely wasn't a soldier. But he took it personally when he heard Goliath mocking God.

The sin and evil we face today come from the same place Goliath's evil did: Satan. Satan's goal is to challenge the people of God every day.

In what ways do you see Satan challenging the people of God today?

How do you respond to evil challenges?

Pray this week that your love for God will cause you to take it seriously when you confront sin.

Day 2
1 Samuel 17:38-51

The odds were against David. Saul tried to place his armor on David, but the only thing that fit him was what David used to fight wild animals—a sling and stones. With just a sling, David entered a fight against a giant who had armor, a spear, a sword, and a javelin.

Of course, the most significant piece of armor David carried wasn't a weapon or a defensive shield. David carried the equalizer—the knockout punch—because he went into battle carrying the name of the Lord.

Isn't it strange that Christians feel so defeated while facing their daily battles when we, too, carry the name of the Lord? Realize you can be victorious when confronting evil because God is on your side.

What battles do you face in your life?

What weapons do you have to face those battles?

How can you trust the name of the Lord as you enter the battle?

Day 3
Psalm 8:1-9

When David was a young shepherd boy, he spent a lot of time alone thinking about God and meditating on God's greatness. The psalm you read today sounds as if it came from those days when David tended sheep in God's great outdoors. David was in awe of the majesty of God.

If it's been a while since you've been confronted with God's majesty, then it's time to get alone with your heavenly Father. If weather permits, and if you have a quiet place to go outside, then try to have a time of devotion outdoors today.

Compare yourself with David and the time he spent alone with God. How is your devotion to God similar to David's?

How is your devotion to God different from David's?

Thank God for his creation and for making himself known to you.

Day 4
2 Samuel 7:8-16

God's promises can sometimes stretch into eternity. God promised David that his kingdom would last forever. And while it's true that David's descendants were kings in Jerusalem for hundreds of years after David's death, that wasn't really the fulfillment of this promise.

God didn't mean just 10, 50, 100, or 1,000 years. He literally meant eternity—for all time. And God's promise to David was ultimately realized when Jesus—one of David's descendants—died on a cross and rose again to establish God's eternal kingdom in heaven. Jesus will reign for all eternity.

Thank God for the wonderful promise of eternal life with him.

Day 5
2 Samuel 7:18-26

After God made a covenant with him, David was in awe that God loved him and did so much for him. When David considered the greatness of God, he was struck by his own comparative smallness. When he realized the God of all creation was personally concerned about him, David said, "There is no one like you, and there is no God but you" (verse 22).

God has done much in your life. Are you as overwhelmed by his love and grace as David was? Or have you learned to take the greatness of God for granted? If you can really catch a glimpse of God's vastness—how totally amazing he is—then you'll be caught up in awe of God just as David was.

How do you feel when you compare yourself with God's greatness?

How do you feel when you consider that God loves you deeply—even though he's so significant and you're so small? Make some notes about these thoughts as you journal today.

Praise God that even in his great majesty he loves you even more than you'll ever comprehend.

WEEK 31
KING DAVID: THE DEVASTATION OF SIN

MEMORY VERSES

"Do you not know that your body is a temple of the Holy Spirit, who is in you, whom you have received from God? You are not your own; you were bought at a price. Therefore honor God with your body." (1 Corinthians 6:19-20)

INTRODUCTION

Psalm 101 was written during David's younger years. In it he spells out his position on holy living. He wrote that he'd be careful to lead a blameless life by staying away from evil. He also declared he'd keep a protective eye on the godly and not allow liars to enter his presence. David went so far as to proclaim that even those who served him would have to live a life above reproach.

When David reached middle adulthood, his high standards started to erode. One look at a beautiful woman and David quickly became an adulterer, a deceiver, and eventually a murderer. Sadly, he fell into a pattern of sin without feeling much guilt. Finally, when the prophet Nathan confronted him about his evil ways, David confessed his sin and repented. That's the end of the story, right? Wrong.

Today the entertainment industry floods television, movies, and music with stories of people sinning and suffering no consequences. That's not reality. David was forgiven, but he had to deal with family problems that resulted from his sin, including the death of some of his children and a rebellious son who almost cost him his throne. Look at David's later years if you believe sin comes without a high cost.

Sin is a big deal to God. God forgives freely, but negative consequences for sinful actions still affect not only you and those around you now, but also future generations. As it's been said, you're free to choose your actions, but you're not free to choose the consequences of your actions. How you deal with sin is one of the most important decisions you'll make as a Christian.

DAILY DEVOTIONS

Day 1
2 Samuel 11:2-17

David's sin with Bathsheba led to deception and eventually the murder of her husband, Uriah.

Sin follows a predictable pattern: First, the act itself, then the cover-up, and then more deception. For instance, let's say you go to a party your parents told you not to go to. Since you don't want your parents to find out about it, you lie and tell them you were with a friend. Then you have to get that friend involved in your lie by telling her to go along with your story—just in case your parents say something. Next, you have to concoct another story about what you and your friend were doing that night, and so on.

Obviously, every sin won't lead to murder. In fact, one of Satan's best tricks is to make us feel as if we got away with sin. That way sin will seem to be less of a problem the next time we're tempted. But sin weaves a deadly web. If we allow it to build up in our lives, it will destroy our reputation, cause us to lose intimacy with God, and create pain for us and for those around us.

We all fail. We're all given to sin. The key is not to allow sin to go unchecked. Confess and repent of it.

Pray—not only this week, but also daily—that God will forgive the sins you've committed against him. Ask him to guard your heart so you don't allow sin to take root in your life.

Day 2
2 Samuel 12:1-12

Sin has a blinding effect that can cause us not to see the seriousness of our actions. In fact, we can get so engrossed in it that we begin to have an easy time justifying it. We may even begin to have a hard time seeing it as sin. Sometimes it takes a serious wake-up call to jolt us back to reality.

King David's wake-up call came when the prophet Nathan told him an emotional story about the theft of a lamb. When David became angry at the injustice, Nathan pointed his finger at David and spoke these penetrating words: "You are the man." Those words from Nathan must have struck David like a knife to the heart.

When have you experienced a wake-up call about your own sin?

Is there anything in your life that you need a wake-up call for now? What is it?

Pray today that you'll always be sensitive and aware of your sin—no matter what it takes to do so.

Day 3
Psalm 32

David wrote this psalm out of his own experience. His sin made him miserable, but his joy returned when he realized God had cleared his record. Joy is the result of living a life of honesty before God.

No one will be able to go through life without sinning. What you do after you sin is really important. If you confess your sins to God, then you can live a life of honesty and experience joy in your daily walk with God.

Are you feeling close to God today? If not, is there unconfessed sin in your life?

Pray right now, confess your sin, and ask for God's forgiveness and restoration.

Day 4
Psalm 101

In this passage we can see that as a young man, David had very high standards for his life that flowed out of his relationship with God. But as an adult, he violated the principles and convictions he once wrote about for a few minutes of sexual pleasure. How sad.

When you live today's Scripture passage, you'll have raised the bar of character in your own life. But when you make a mistake in some way and sin, ask for forgiveness and get right back to living a godly life.

Here's a tough question to consider: If you compromise a conviction, then was it ever a conviction in the first place?

Pray that you'll hold firm to your convictions and not compromise them for any type of temptation—as David did.

Day 5
2 Samuel 12:13-21

David sinned, asked forgiveness, and then had to live with the consequences of his sin. Satan would like you to believe sinful living has no price tag. He wants you to think, A little of this...a little of that...it never hurt anyone. But he's totally deceiving you. Are you buying it? While it's true that all sin is totally forgivable (except for rejecting Christ), the consequences can last a long time. They certainly did for King David.

Are you currently involved in any sin that has no consequences?

Stop and think for a moment: What's the best thing that can happen if you continue in this sin? What's the worst thing?

Pray earnestly that God will help you get out of this sin and that he'll forgive you as you repent of it. He will.

WEEK 32
KING SOLOMON: THE DANGERS OF PROSPERITY

MEMORY VERSE

"For where your treasure is, there your heart will be also." (Matthew 6:21)

INTRODUCTION

Have you ever thought about what you'd ask for if you were granted a wish? King Solomon was given an opportunity to ask God for anything.

Solomon became the king of Israel after the death of his father, David. One night during a dream, God appeared to Solomon and told him to ask for whatever he wanted. Without hesitation Solomon told God he wanted wisdom to govern and to know the difference between right and wrong. Because God was so pleased with the request, he gave Solomon both wisdom and riches.

Solomon's reputation for being a man of wisdom quickly spread throughout the world. Soon people flocked to ask the king for wise counsel. Solomon's wisdom grew and so did his wealth and fame. He had wealth, and he had 1,000 beautiful women as his wives and concubines. But that's where the trouble started. All of those foreign women led Solomon to ungodly worship. By the time he was an old man, his heart had turned away from God. The wisest man who ever lived did the most unwise thing: He allowed his heart to turn from God.

Jesus warned about the dangers of prosperity. Paul said the love of money is the root of all kinds of evil (1 Timothy 6:10). Solomon lost his perspective and allowed what he had to become more important than what he believed. Jesus said, "For where your treasure is, there your heart will be also" (Matthew 6:21).

DAILY DEVOTIONS

Day 1
1 Kings 3:3-14

Solomon had the opportunity of a lifetime—to ask God for whatever he wanted. What would you ask for? Wealth? Power? Fame? Solomon could have asked for those things. Instead, he asked for wisdom. Why wisdom? Solomon desired to be a good king, and he knew he'd need God's wisdom to lead God's people. So God granted his request and gave Solomon great wisdom. Many of Solomon's wise sayings are found in the book of Proverbs.

Read James 1:5. Isn't that amazing? God is asking you to ask him for the very same thing Solomon did—wisdom. And God promises that if you approach him in faith when you ask for his wisdom, he'll give it to you.

What would you ask God for if you were given the opportunity to ask him for anything?

Would your request be a wise or an unwise wish?

What wisdom do you need in your life right now?

As you pray today, ask God to grant you wisdom to deal with the things going on in your life right now.

Day 2
1 Kings 10:23-25

Solomon's wisdom was known throughout the world. People came from all over to ask for Solomon's advice, and he used the gift God had given him to make a difference in the lives of many people. It's one thing to receive a gift from God; it's quite another thing to use that gift in his service.

Sometimes we take our gifts for granted; we make no special effort to use them for God. God may have blessed you in any number of ways, given you material wealth, musical ability, athletic ability, or the ability to make friends easily. Are you using the things God has given you to honor him?

Think about what gifts, abilities, and talents God has given you. What are some of them?

Are you purposefully using those things to bring glory to him?

Day 3
1 Kings 11:1-13

Solomon failed because he disobeyed God and married women who worshiped false gods. Solomon's life is proof that, outside of accepting Christ, choosing the person you'll marry will definitely be the most important decision you'll ever make and will have the most influence and impact on your life. You can be wise in every area of your life and still completely fail if you tie yourself to a person (or persons) who leads you away from God.

Pray today that God will give you wisdom when it comes to choosing whom you'll date and ultimately whom you will marry.

Day 4
Proverbs 1:1-7

What did a man known for his wisdom have to say about wisdom? Solomon said that if you want wisdom, you must begin by having a healthy fear of the Lord. The words fear of God don't mean you're to be "afraid" of God in the same way you'd fear a murderer or a hurricane.

Think about it: Why would a God whom we're to love, honor, and serve want us to live in fear of him? No, the word fear in this context means we're to respect and honor him. We're to fear God as a son might fear a father who is full of love for him, but willing to punish him if he fails to obey. Solomon realized God was the source of his spiritual wisdom.

Do you have a proper fear of God in the sense Solomon wrote about?

What can you point to in your life that proves this?

Pray that God will show you what it means to show proper honor and respect to him in your daily life.

Day 5
Proverbs 4:14-27

What would Solomon say to today's teenager about following God? According to today's Scripture passage, Solomon's advice would be not to follow the crowd, to stay in God's Word, to guard your heart, and to keep your eyes on God. Solomon learned these lessons the hard way—through his own failures. Put Solomon's advice to work in your life and stay strong as a Christian teenager.

How many of the above spiritual disciplines are you actively involved in right now?

How could you use more of these disciplines in your life?

Even though Solomon wrote these words thousands of years ago, following his advice will help you live fully as a 21st-century teenager.

WEEK 33
PROPHET ELIJAH: THE PROVISION OF GOD

MEMORY VERSE

"For the jar of flour was not used up and the jug of oil did not run dry, in keeping with the word of the Lord spoken by Elijah." (1 Kings 17:16)

INTRODUCTION

When Solomon died, the nation of Israel was shattered. Israel was made up of 12 tribes—each composed of the descendants of one of Jacob's sons. The 10 northern tribes refused to follow Solomon's son Rehoboam. They chose Jeroboam as their king and abandoned the southern tribe of Judah. Meanwhile, Judah (along with the much smaller tribe of Benjamin) remained loyal to Solomon's son.

During this time of political tension, God began to raise up prophets to speak his words against the sins of the people. God spoke to the prophets in various ways, but each prophet was called to proclaim God's words to his people.

The prophet Elijah prophesied against the wicked King Ahab of the northern kingdom (Israel) and ended up fleeing for his life. God sent a drought to the region. Eventually, God sent Elijah to a poor widow in the village of Zarephath. When Elijah asked her for bread, she told him she was down to her last bit of flour. Elijah told her if she'd bake him a small loaf of bread from her tiny supply of flour, God would provide for her and her son. The widow acted in faith, and God miraculously refilled her flour container each time she prepared a meal. When her son later died, the power of God brought the boy back to life.

God is always providing for his people. Sometimes we overlook the provision of God until we face difficult times. God took care of Elijah. He took care of the widow and her son. And he'll take care of you.

DAILY DEVOTIONS

Day 1
1 Kings 16:29-34

Think about the people in your life who influence you. Your list may include your parents, close friends, people at church, or fictional characters on television. Influence is a powerful thing. It can be a very positive force in your life. Because of the influence of a science teacher, a student might become a researcher who discovers the cure for an awful disease. Unfortunately, influence can also be negative. Too many teenagers have discovered too late that their friends' encouragement to see how fast their cars could go was bad advice.

Unfortunately for King Ahab, he was greatly influenced by his pagan wife, Jezebel. He set up a shrine and temple for Baal as a result of Jezebel's influence, and he was ultimately named to God's list of evil kings.

Are you an influencee (being influenced by others—especially nonbelievers) or an influencer (influencing others for God)? Be honest.

What influences do you need to eliminate from your life?

In what ways do you need to become more of an influencer?
Pray this week that God will help you to be a person of godly influence.

Day 2
1 Kings 17:1-7

After boldly standing before King Ahab and telling him God was sending a drought, Elijah went and hid in a ravine just as God instructed. God provided ravens that brought Elijah food each day and a brook for drinking water. Can you imagine having birds bring you food? How did the ravens do it? What did they bring? We don't know, but we do know God provided just what Elijah needed. That's the most important thing to remember from this passage.

If God is always the same and if he took care of Elijah, then don't you think you can be confident that God will take care of you?

Are you facing a situation in which you don't know how God will provide? What's the situation? What do you need from God?

Trust God and see what he'll do.

Day 3
1 Kings 17:8-16

God told Elijah to go to a widow's house in Zarephath and give her a faith test. Because she gave part of her last bit of food to the prophet, God provided food for her and her son. He also allowed Elijah to bring her only son back to life after he'd died.

Having faith in God—and then acting on that faith—is powerful. Sometimes it unleashes God's miraculous power.

Would you pass a faith test from God? Why or why not?

What would you have to change about the way you live—the way you see life—in order to pass a faith test?

Ask God to help you adjust your life to live as the widow of Zarephath did.

Day 4
Psalm 95:1-11

The reference to God as a shepherd is an excellent example of how he provides for us. A shepherd will do whatever it takes to protect and care for his sheep. He sleeps with one eye open, he protects them from wild animals, he leads them to green pastures, and he rescues those who become lost. That's how God treats us because he watches over us like sheep under his care.

What are some benefits to having God be like a shepherd to us?

Thank God today that he's watching over you as a caring shepherd.

Day 5
Matthew 6:25-34

The most important part of all of God's creation is you. What? Yes, you! Jesus said that if God will take care of the birds (which are actually of little value), then he'll surely take care of you. And if he can beautifully clothe the lilies of the field (which are pretty but of no eternal value), think of how much he must love and care for you.

You're his greatest creation. Just think about it: If God is there to provide for and protect us every hour of every day, then we really don't have any worries.

Have you ever thought much about being God's choice creation?

Understanding how much God cares for you should cause you to love and honor him more. It should also help you consider the lengths God goes to in order to take care of you.

Thank God today that you're his crowning creation and that God will provide for you.

WEEK 34
PROPHET ELIJAH: NEVER ALONE

MEMORY VERSES

"Elijah was a man just like us. He prayed earnestly that it would not rain, and it did not rain on the land for three and a half years. Again he prayed, and the heavens gave rain, and the earth produced its crops." (James 5:17-18)

INTRODUCTION

Sports fans love great matchups like an all-star pitcher facing a home-run hitter or a great quarterback taking on a top defensive team. Sometimes the encounters become legendary—basketball's Larry Bird playing against Magic Johnson, or Muhammad Ali boxing Joe Frazier.

The Old Testament includes a story about a battle of historic proportions, and if they'd had big stadiums back then, this event would have been a sellout.

Elijah was fed up with the way the Israelites were wavering between worshiping God and Baal. So on famous Mount Carmel, Elijah challenged the prophets of the false god. Big crowds gathered to watch 450 of Baal's prophets attempt to get their god to burn up a sacrifice. Then it was Elijah's turn. God answered his two-sentence prayer, and fire fell from heaven.

Because Queen Jezebel was a big follower of Baal, she vowed to have Elijah killed after he embarrassed the prophets of her god. So Elijah ran for his life. Then, despite his victory on Mount Carmel, his fear of Jezebel caused Elijah to feel depressed and alone. He even prayed for God to take his life. During that time God ministered to Elijah and helped him see he wasn't alone. God was with him at all times.

Today, we have something available to us that Elijah didn't have in his day: The Holy Spirit of God living in us. When we feel sad and lonely like Elijah did, we don't have to ask God to appear for our comfort, because he already lives in us. And that's a comfort you can always depend on.

DAILY DEVOTIONS

Day 1
1 Kings 18:16-21

A confrontation was brewing. King Ahab had led the people to worship the false god Baal, and now the Israelites were divided in their loyalties. They were trying to follow both God and Baal. So Elijah confronted their divided hearts. Read again what he told them in verse 21.

God deserves absolute commitment from his people. He doesn't want lip service. He calls us to live differently from the lost world around us. Just as God's people in the time of Elijah had to make a choice, so do you.

In what ways do you have divided loyalties—sometimes following God, sometimes following the world?

What do you need to do today to choose to follow only God?

Ask God to reveal to you any areas of your life that you haven't totally given to him.

Day 2
1 Kings 18:22-29

For six long hours, the prophets of Baal shouted, danced themselves into a frenzy, and even cut themselves trying to get the attention of their god. He never answered them. Of course, the problem was their god didn't exist. It's easy to sit back and laugh at the foolishness of the Baal worshipers; but if you're not careful, you can make the same mistake they made. You can seek after the illusions the world has to offer—fame, money, looks—while all the time God is waiting to give you real power for living.

Do you sometimes find yourself buying into illusions? If so, what are they?

As you survey your life, how are you doing at focusing your attention on the real God and avoiding the deceptions of the false gods of our time?

Ask God to help you be faithful in following him and turn your back on the false gods you may be tempted to serve.

Day 3
1 Kings 18:30-40

I stood by Niagara Falls and was mesmerized by the sheer force and power of all that water. Sometimes you can see a hint of God's power and glory as you look at what he's made. But all the water of Niagara is literally a drop in the bucket when compared with the power of God.

When Elijah called to God, fire fell from heaven. It consumed the altars of sacrifice, the wood, and even the water. There was no doubt God had shown up. The people's only response was to fall on their faces and shout, "The Lord he is God!" That was the appropriate response given what they'd just seen.

Can you think of a time when you were confronted with the power of God? Write about that experience on this page.

Even if you cannot name a specific Mount Carmel experience, God is still at work around you. Thank him for his power and presence in your life.

Day 4
1 Kings 19:9-18

The big show was over. God had done amazing things on Mount Carmel. After Elijah came down from the mountain, he suddenly seemed different—not the incredible man of God he'd shown himself to be as he faced the priests of Baal. When Jezebel threatened Elijah's very life, he fled, feeling alone and depressed.

You may have experienced a letdown similar to Elijah's. Unfortunately, a mountaintop experience can soon be followed by a trip to a valley. One day, you feel closer to God than ever; the next day you feel alone and helpless. The thing to remember in those times is that the God of the mountain is also the God of the valley. God is still in control, and he still loves you. God ministered to Elijah when he was down, and he'll do the same for you.

What are you facing right now that has you feeling down?

What do you need to say to God about it? Make some notes in your journal space.

Remember: God will give you the strength you need to make it through.

Day 5
Psalm 57:1-11

David knew exactly how Elijah felt; he wrote this psalm feeling much the same way. He, too, had run for his life (from King Saul). David had also hidden in a cave. But David offered an interesting solution to loneliness and fear: Thank God and praise him. What? Yes, David discovered that an attitude of thanks and praise was great medicine for a fearful heart.

How do you usually respond to being afraid or threatened? Do you tend to get angry or to retreat?

How could you remember to turn your attention to praising and thanking God when you feel alone, tired, or fearful?

WEEK 35
PROPHET ELISHA: EQUIPPED FOR GOD'S PURPOSE

MEMORY VERSE

"The one who calls you is faithful and he will do it." (1 Thessalonians 5:24)

INTRODUCTION

I remember the first time I was asked to fill in for the morning disc jockey at a local Christian radio station. I'd been a DJ in the 1980s, but today's technology made radio a new adventure. The regular morning person taught me the basic computer skills for the job. He prepared me well, but I was still nervous on my first day. I made a few mistakes, but the training helped me keep the station on the air for four hours.

Elijah was a mentor to Elisha. While Elijah was hiding out from Queen Jezebel, God told him to anoint Elisha as the next prophet. The two men spent 10 years together. When God took Elijah to heaven in a chariot of fire, Elisha was left to carry on the work.

When the time came for Elisha to do God's work without his mentor, Elisha picked up Elijah's cloak and struck the water of the Jordan River. The water parted, and the people watching knew God had called Elisha to be Elijah's successor.

God performed many miracles through Elisha; but most importantly, Elisha always spoke God's words in God's time.

You may be fortunate enough to have a mentor to train you to fulfill God's call on your life. Perhaps your mentor is your youth minister or your parent. But the day will come when you must step out on your own and do God's work. You can trust God; he'll never call you to a task without giving you what you need to accomplish it.

DAILY DEVOTIONS

Day 1
1 Kings 19:19-21

Considering the number of oxen Elisha had, he must have been fairly wealthy. When Elijah called him to be a "prophet in training," Elisha not only left his parents, but he also slaughtered his oxen and set fire to his plow to cook the meat. Why? He got rid of all his possessions so he'd have nothing to go back to. Elisha gave up everything to follow God.

Are you holding on to a safety net—something you can go back to if you decide not to follow God? What parts of your life before Christ do you keep around just in case you want to go back to them?

Pray this week that God will ignite in your soul the kind of passion Elisha had.

Day 2
2 Kings 2:5-12

After 10 years of mentoring Elisha, the time came for Elijah to leave. Before taking off in a chariot of fire, however, Elijah asked Elisha what he could do for him. Instead of asking Elijah to bless him with some type of worldly gain, Elisha asked for a double portion of the prophet Elijah's spirit. Elisha longed for the passionate obedience to God that he'd seen in his mentor's life. He longed to be used by God as Elijah had been.

How passionate are you about your spiritual life?

Is there anyone you long to be like because of his rich relationship with God? Who?

How do you see that relationship with God exhibited in his life?

Pray that you'll seek to be an Elisha.

Day 3
2 Kings 2:13-18

Elijah's cloak was symbolic of the power of God. When Elisha touched the water with the cloak, the river parted. The miracle convinced a group of prophets that Elisha was more than a friend of Elijah; he was the one who'd continue Elijah's work. This miracle probably confirmed the same truth for Elisha, too. God would use Elisha as his mouthpiece to his people.

William Carey, the eighteenth- and nineteenth-century preacher and missionary to India, said we should "expect great things from God and attempt great things for God." That can be done only through God's power.

Have you ever thought about God's power resting on you—or in you?

That doesn't necessarily mean you'll be able to do superhuman feats of strength, but it does mean you have the most powerful force in the universe—God's Spirit—inside of you.

What's happened in your life that can be explained only by the power of God?

Ask God for the courage to attempt things only God can let you accomplish.

Day 4
2 Kings 4:1-7

This is one of 13 miracles God did through the prophet Elisha. (Read 2 Kings 2–13 to discover the other 12 miracles.) God's power was strong in Elisha's life because he was available to God and obedient to God.

God's power is available to you. He probably won't do the miracles in your life that he did through Elisha. After all, God performed those particular miracles only once. But God can use you to make a difference in the world around you. As you experience God's power, you'll begin to see the world as he sees it. You'll be quicker to pray and quicker to act when you see a need.

If God's power isn't evident in your life, check your desire to be available and obedient to God. In what ways do you believe you've experienced God's power in the past?

How willing are you to be used by God?

Ask God to give you wisdom to understand what it means to have his power.

Day 5
2 Kings 13:20-21

This is an amazing story about God's power at work in Elisha. Some Israelites were burying a dead man, and a group of raiders started heading their way, so the Israelites threw the body into Elisha's tomb. The power of God was so great in Elisha that contact with his dead bones brought this dead man back to life.

If God can use dry, old bones in such a miraculous way, think of what he can do with a living teenager. He can use you to do incredible things. Think of the people you know who are spiritually dead. A dead man coming back to life after touching Elisha's bones was truly miraculous, but that man died again. If God uses you to bring a person to life spiritually by helping her know Christ, then she'll be alive with God for eternity.

Whom can you touch with God's power?

Make a commitment to give God your all. See what he'll do through you.

WEEK 36
PROPHET HOSEA: UNFAILING LOVE

MEMORY VERSE

"For I desire mercy, not sacrifice, and acknowledgment of God rather than burnt offerings." (Hosea 6:6)

INTRODUCTION

Hosea is the subject of one of the greatest love stories in the Bible. And he was one of God's prophets. Hosea was called to prophesy during the days before Israel was destroyed. God also asked him to do something very unusual. Hosea's obedience to God sent a strong message about the loyal, unconditional love of God.

The ministry of Hosea extended 45 years. He lived his early life in the prosperous land of Israel, but the sin of the people caused conditions in the country to deteriorate. The main sin Hosea speaks of in his book is idolatry. As a way to demonstrate the relationship between God and his people, God told Hosea to marry a prostitute by the name of Gomer. She was unfaithful and left Hosea. Later he found her on the slave market and restored her as his wife.

Hosea and Gomer represent God and Israel. Just as Hosea chose a sinner to be his wife, God chose Israel to be his chosen people. As Gomer was unfaithful to Hosea, Israel was unfaithful to God by worshiping idols. Hosea redeemed Gomer because of his love. That was a picture of God always loving his people with perfect love.

Have you ever tried to love someone who's hurt you? Maybe you were hurt by a parent, a relative, or a friend. Hosea felt that same pain. It's the same pain God feels. Our usual response to someone who hurts us is to stop loving that person. That wasn't what Hosea did, and that isn't how God responds to us. Be thankful for God's unconditional love. As a Christian, practice unconditional love in your day-to-day relationships.

DAILY DEVOTIONS

Day 1
Hosea 1

Speaking for God doesn't really cost me that much—study time and prayer time are important, but the cost to me isn't really that huge.

For Hosea it was different. Hosea's whole life was a picture of God's redemption and love. Can you imagine anything more humiliating than being told by God to marry a prostitute? But Hosea obeyed God. His life became his message. God used Hosea's relationship with this prostitute as a human illustration. God's people—the Israelites—were committing the vilest spiritual adultery by worshiping other gods. Despite their spiritual adultery, God continued to love them.

God will probably never call you to marry a prostitute. (Hosea is the only person in Scripture to receive that particular call.) However, God may call you to do difficult things, such as risk your reputation or popularity, or make personal sacrifices. Following Christ isn't always easy, but it's always worth it.

Have you ever had to suffer for something God called you to do? If so, what was it?

Pray that God will help you move toward complete obedience to him—even if his ways don't make sense to you.

Day 2
Hosea 3

It hurts when someone you love rejects you. Hosea's marriage wasn't just an object lesson for him; Gomer was his wife, and he gave her his heart. She was unfaithful and deceitful. Nevertheless, God told Hosea to reconcile with Gomer—to love her despite her adultery and apparent lack of love for him. God was painting a picture of his love for his chosen people—and Israel's repeated rejection of him.

God's love is always forgiving. His love is also completely undeserved. That's God's grace to us. You'll never be good enough for God, but he loves you unconditionally. You may have rebelled against him again and again through sin, but God always forgives you and draws you back to himself. He doesn't draw you back to allow you to stay in sin but so you can have fellowship with him.

What are some ways you've shown yourself to be unfaithful to God?

How have you experienced his love when you've been unfaithful?

Thank God today for his faithful, reconciling, and redeeming love.

Day 3
Hosea 14:1-9

Real forgiveness is hard. Imagine someone does something to hurt you. You can say, "That's okay; don't worry about it." But then you cringe every time you see that person for the next month. Real forgiveness isn't "I'll forgive you if..." Real forgiveness means giving up the right to mention the offense the next time you get mad. Real forgiveness isn't easy.

God's way of forgiving is forgetting about the offense forever and then healing the relationship with his perfect love. That's the kind of forgiveness the human heart longs for. We know we've failed. We know we need forgiveness. God forgives.

Is there someone you need to forgive? Who is it and what's the reason?

Ask God to help you forgive and reach out in love.

Day 4
John 13:31-35

As Jesus was preparing to go to the cross, he wanted to leave his disciples with a new commandment. The Jewish law stressed loving God; Jesus said to take love to a higher level and show God's love to other people. In fact, he said others would know we're his disciples if we love each other. Yes, we're to love God. The most significant way to express love to God is to love other people—even the unlovable.

Evaluate your discipleship by your level of love for others. How good a disciple are you?

Day 5
1 Corinthians 13:1-13

Faith, hope, and love—according to Paul, all three will last forever. So they must all be important, right? Which is most important? The apostle Paul didn't hesitate: The greatest of the three is love. Maybe Paul considered love the greatest because love not only compels us to minister to other people, but it's also the best way to express the very nature of God.

If you want other people to see and experience God through your life and actions, the way to do so is simple: Love them.

How would you grade yourself in the area of loving others?

What do you need to do to improve your grade?

Ask God to teach you what it means to really love others.

WEEK 37
PROPHET ISAIAH: "I SAW THE LORD"

MEMORY VERSE

"Then I heard the voice of the Lord saying, 'Whom shall I send? And who will go for us?' And I said, 'Here am I. Send me!'" (Isaiah 6:8)

INTRODUCTION

You may remember an experience with God that changed your life. Maybe you had an encounter with him at a youth camp, on a mission trip, or during a special service at your church. Wherever it happened, a powerful experience with God is unforgettable and life changing. That's how it was when the prophet Isaiah encountered God.

Isaiah was a prophet in Judah, the southern kingdom. He received his call from God through a direct vision. In his vision Isaiah saw the holiness of God, and he became intensely aware of his own sin. When God cleansed him of his sins, Isaiah was ready to accept God's challenge to be his messenger.

Isaiah was a prominent figure in the Old Testament. His words continued to have influence in the New Testament. He ministered more than 40 years in Judah, and during that time he gave many specific prophecies about the coming Messiah—prophecies that Jesus would fulfill more than 600 years later. Isaiah is quoted more than 50 times in the New Testament, yet his words fell on deaf ears while he was alive. His death was cruel: He was sawed in half during the reign of the wicked Manasseh.

If you understand Isaiah, then you'll see worship differently. In God's presence Isaiah received a mission from God. Isaiah was faithful to God's call until the day he died. You've probably experienced times of worship when God seemed near and powerful. In times like that, you can count on God's holiness convicting you of sin. Then get ready to receive a glimpse of God's call on your life.

DAILY DEVOTIONS

Day 1
Isaiah 6:1-4

We're going to take this week's devotions slowly because of this chapter's beauty.

In today's passage Isaiah had a vision of the absolute holiness of God. One Bible scholar believes the reason the angels sang each time they circled God was because they always encountered a different aspect of God's awesome nature.

God has so many attributes that listing them all is difficult. What an awesome God we serve! When you worship God, privately or with a group, try to picture the attributes of the One you worship. He is merciful, good, joyful, righteous, and holy.

Describe a time when your worship of God was overwhelming to you.

What aspects of God's character have come to mean the most to you?

Spend a few minutes worshiping God for who he is today.

Day 2
Isaiah 6:5

Think about what it's like to get up in the middle of the night. You stumble through the darkness to the bathroom. You can probably see enough to avoid the furniture because of the light shining between the drapes. In fact, the house may not seem that dark—until you switch on the light. The blazing light causes you to squeeze your eyes shut. The sudden shock of light is almost painful. Coming into the presence of God is like that.

Today's reading includes just one powerful verse. When people have a genuine encounter with God, they usually become convicted of their sins. True worship leads most of us to the desire to repent. That's probably because the closer we get to God, the more aware we become of our own sins and shortcomings in his presence. That's exactly what happened to the prophet Isaiah.

Have you ever had an experience with God that made you keenly aware of your sin? When was it?

How did you respond to God?

Pray that God will give you a strong desire to respond to him now.

Day 3
Isaiah 6:6-7

When Isaiah became aware of his sin, God made a way to forgive that sin. An angel touched Isaiah's mouth with a hot coal. The picture is clear—the unclean words Isaiah admitted to were burned away.

Forgiveness and cleansing from sin are available to you. The cost for you to be forgiven has already been paid. Your sins were forgiven when Jesus died on the cross for you. Ask God for forgiveness, and you'll get it. That's a promise from God himself.

Memorize the following verse today if you haven't already done so:

> If we confess our sins, he is faithful and just and will forgive us our sins and purify us from all unrighteousness. (1 John 1:9)

Thank God for the forgiveness he provides for us through Jesus.

Day 4
Isaiah 6:8

God's communication with his people is a little like a radio signal. Every hour of every day radio signals are broadcast all around us, but the only time we hear them is when we have a radio turned on. We miss a lot of what God is trying to say to us because we aren't tuned in to his signal.

Keep your spiritual radio on by staying intimate with God—on a continuing basis. If you really liked listening to the radio, you wouldn't simply turn it on for a few minutes in the morning and then turn it off for the rest of the day. The same is true for communicating with God. The more we stay in touch with him, the more ready we are to say—as Isaiah did—"Here am I, send me!"

How is your communication with God? Is it such that if he were to speak instructions to you, you could hear and then obey?

If not, what's keeping you from this type of relationship with him?

Tell God you're ready to do what he wants you to do. You'll never regret doing so.

Day 5
Isaiah 6:9-13

Unfortunately for Isaiah, he was called to preach a message that fell on deaf ears. Isaiah's success wasn't in results; it was in his faithful obedience to tell the people what God told him to say.

You may be called to a task that has no visible measure of success. Remember, God isn't looking for you to get things done. He desires your obedience.

Which is more important to you—popularity or obedience to God?

Ask God for an obedient heart.

WEEK 38
KING HEZEKIAH: REPENTANCE AND DELIVERANCE

MEMORY VERSE

"Hezekiah trusted in the Lord, the God of Israel. There was no one like him among all the kings of Judah, either before him or after him." (2 Kings 18:5)

INTRODUCTION

Israel was divided. The northern kingdom was still called Israel, and the southern kingdom was called Judah. The spiritual climate of both kingdoms was determined largely by the king in power. Some kings were good and led the people to worship the true God; other kings were evil and led the people away from God. Hezekiah was a good king.

Hezekiah ruled Judah for 29 years. He removed pagan shrines and led the people to worship God. A lot of good things were happening in Judah, but then trouble started brewing. Assyria conquered Israel, and then the king of Assyria set his sights on Judah.

The king of Assyria attempted to intimidate Hezekiah with a letter detailing his military victories. Hezekiah knew Israel had been taken into exile by Assyria, and Judah was now facing the same fate. But Hezekiah prayed God would rescue Judah from Assyria so everyone would know the Lord alone was God.

Soon, the prophet Isaiah visited Hezekiah and told him God had heard his prayer; Assyria wouldn't overtake them. God sent an angel to the Assyrian camp and killed 185,000 troops. When the Assyrians woke the next day and saw the dead bodies, they quickly returned to their homeland. And when the Assyrian king got home, his two sons killed him in the temple of his pagan god. God is always bigger than anything this world can throw at those who truly trust in him.

DAILY DEVOTIONS

Day 1
2 Kings 17:7-17

The northern kingdom allowed pagan temples to be built. They intermarried with the pagan people who lived around them. They trusted their alliances rather than trusting God. Even God's chosen people sacrificed their own children, consulted fortune-tellers, and used witchcraft. The path of sin is a downward spiral, and it can lead only to destruction. Ultimately, Israel was destroyed by outside enemies because of the sins of the people.

Sin never starts with human sacrifice. It begins with little compromises. Little by little, people allow more sin into their lives. God calls people to repent. If they do, he forgives. If they don't, more serious consequences will follow. The experiences of Israel should teach us to take sin seriously. If you don't seek God and keep sin in check, it can destroy your life.

Pray that God will convict you of your sins. Then ask him for forgiveness daily.

Day 2
2 Kings 18:1-8

There are many definitions of success. King Hezekiah removed pagan idols, obeyed God's commands, and was faithful to him. The result of all this was that God was with him, and Hezekiah became successful in all he did.

But the world's definition of success is usually not the same as God's definition. If your desire is to be a success in life (or in anything you do), make certain you follow God's definition and not the world's. We owe the world nothing; we owe God everything.

In what areas do you hope to succeed?

Are those worldly or godly views of success?

If they're worldly views, what do you need to do to change your perspective to pursue godly views of success?

Day 3
2 Kings 19:8-16

The king of Assyria wanted to invade Judah, and he tried to intimidate King Hezekiah by proudly telling of all his conquests. The threat was very real. The Assyrian king had proven how mighty his army was. Hezekiah's response was to take the matter to God in prayer. On paper Hezekiah was no match for the Assyrian army. But Hezekiah had faith that God would be his protection.

As a Christian, you'll usually be in the minority in this world. Unbelievers probably surround you at school. You may even be the only believer in your home. But don't ever be intimidated by those around you. Be like Hezekiah: Take all your situations to God in prayer.

When do you feel intimidated by the world?

How are you able to find faith in God when you feel overwhelmed by the world?
Remember this great saying: You plus God is a majority. You and God are bigger than anything the world can throw at you.

Day 4
2 Kings 19:32-37

Do you really believe God is powerful? We typically say we do, but do we really? God created the world and everything in it. That's pretty powerful. Today's passage tells of God destroying 185,000 Assyrian troops in one night.

God's power is the same today as it was when he created the world and when he destroyed 185,000 Assyrian troops. You can have confidence the powerful God you believe in will take care of you. Even though you may not see the mighty hand of God destroy enemy troops before your eyes, he's all-powerful.

Pray that God will reveal his power in your life when you need it.

Day 5
2 Kings 20:1-11

Toward the end of Hezekiah's life, God performed two big miracles. Miracle 1: Hezekiah was sick and about to die. God sent Isaiah to tell him to get his house in order. In other words, Hezekiah needed to get his will up to date. Death was at his doorstep. So Hezekiah asked God to heal him; God heard his prayer, and before Isaiah left Hezekiah's palace, God sent him back to the king with a different message: Hezekiah would be healed and live another 15 years.

Miracle 2: God provided evidence that he'd give Hezekiah those extra years by making time go in reverse! Apparently, the sun shone in a window that hit the stairs of the palace. As the sun set, the shadow would creep down the stairs. So as a sign from God, the shadow began to go back up the steps. Apparently, the sun was rising when it should have been setting.

God is a God of miracles, and he's still doing miraculous things today.

Can you name a time when you experienced a miracle from God?

God works miracles in our lives every day. Sometimes they're in the things we can see; sometimes they're in the things we cannot see. Thank God for his daily miracles.

WEEK 39
PROPHET JONAH: GOD'S COMPASSION

MEMORY VERSE

"To the roots of the mountains I sank down; the earth beneath barred me in forever. But you brought my life up from the pit, O Lord my God." (Jonah 2:6)

INTRODUCTION

The city of Nineveh was the capital of the Assyrian empire. God had seen the wickedness of the Ninevites and was preparing to judge that great city. The Ninevites showed disregard for God. They worshiped false gods. The Assyrians were vicious and did terrible things to their enemies. This evil and barbaric society was about to come under God's judgment. Enter Jonah.

The prophet Jonah was called to announce the judgment of God to Nineveh. He'd have to travel a great distance to get there. The prospect of meeting evil and cruel people face to face didn't appeal to Jonah, so he hopped on a boat and headed in the opposite direction. Running from the call of God may not have been about fear; Jonah may have actually wanted God to destroy Nineveh—the capital city of one of Israel's potential enemies.

Jonah's disobedience led him into a storm at sea and a trip into the belly of a great fish. In the dark and surely believing he'd die, Jonah finally realized that salvation is from God; he had no right to choose who'd hear the Word of the Lord.

When the big fish spit Jonah out, he went to Nineveh and spoke these few simple words: "Forty more days and Nineveh will be overturned" (Jonah 3:4). Those words created such a revival that even the king repented and called all his people to do the same.

Why did God call Jonah to go preach in Nineveh? God loves all people, and he desires that everyone should have an opportunity to hear about him and respond to him. It's not for us to choose who hears about God. We're simply to obey God and run to—not away from—his call.

DAILY DEVOTIONS

Day 1
Jonah 1:1-17

My uncle once wrote a play about the life of Jonah. That drama was performed a couple of summers on the beach in Panama City, Florida, back in the late 1960s. I'll never forget the image of Jonah running down the beach and away from the call of God until he simply vanished into the night.

Nineveh was approximately 500 miles north of where Jonah was when God called him to go there. Instead, Jonah boarded a ship for Tarshish, which was approximately 2,000 miles to the west. That's some serious running from God.

Think: Have you ever tried to run away from God's call? Perhaps you sensed God wanted you to do something that scared you. Perhaps you knew God wanted you to befriend someone who wasn't very receptive. Perhaps you ignored a command of God when you knew exactly what you were supposed to do. If you can think of an example, write about it as you journal.

How successful have you been at running from God so far?

Pray this week that your Christian influence will not vanish and that God will always give you the strength to run toward his call on your life—not away from it.

Day 2
Jonah 2:1-10

For three days and three nights, Jonah was in the belly of that great fish. God gave him plenty of time to do some serious thinking. His prayer in chapter 2 reflects some of the spiritual truths that became clear to Jonah. Jonah realized salvation comes from God alone and that he didn't have the right to pick who'd hear that message by refusing to act on God's call.

God's message of salvation is for everyone. Jonah's message was news of judgment and destruction. The amazing thing is God has called you to tell people good news: God loves them, God wants to forgive them, and God will give them eternal life if they'll turn to him. Each believer has been called to make the amazing love of God known.

Do you ever think some people aren't good enough for you to tell them about Jesus? What kind of people are they?

Who do you know who needs to hear the good news? Make some notes as you journal today.

Pray that God will use Jonah's example to teach you that God loves all of us.

Day 3
Jonah 3:1-10

Revival came to Nineveh through a few simple words uttered by Jonah: "Forty more days and Nineveh will be overturned." It's hard to imagine that just those words could stir up a revival, but that's just what happened.

A few simple words from God will always have a greater impact than many words spoken on your own. Trust God when he directs you to speak his words to your friends. You don't have to be eloquent or know big theological words to tell others about what God did for you through Jesus. Just tell them what he did in your life.

Ask God to give you the words to be a Jonah to those around you.

Day 4
Psalm 119:25-32

In contrast to Jonah running away from God, the psalmist wrote about running toward God's commandments. Jonah's running brought misery to the people on his boat and brought him three dark days and nights inside a fish. The psalmist's running resulted in a greater love for God and a better understanding of him.

Which path would you rather take?

What does it mean to run toward God's commandments?

Ask God to give your heart the desire to run toward him, not away from him.

Day 5
Jonah 4:1-11

It was sad, but true: Jonah was more concerned about the death of a plant that was bringing him relief from the sun than he was about the lives of 120,000 people in Nineveh.

It's certainly easy to get things out of perspective in our spiritual lives. We can quickly become self-centered and start trying to play God. What can you do to keep this from happening? You can be a servant to others, you can obey God, and you can trust him each time he calls you to do something.

Which is more important to you: What you want or what others need?

Ask the Father to teach you how to put the needs of others ahead of what makes you happy.

WEEK 40
KING JOSIAH: RESPONSE TO GOD'S LAW

MEMORY VERSE

"He did what was right in the eyes of the Lord and walked in the ways of his father David, not turning aside to the right or to the left." (2 Chronicles 34:2)

INTRODUCTION

"Change Your World!" "Impact Your Community for Christ!" "Make a Difference!" I'm sure you've heard phrases about making a difference in the world. If you're honest, then you may not be sold on the idea that you could make much of a difference. Can one person really change things? The answer is "yes."

In *The Tipping Point*, Malcolm Gladwell points out how one person can make a huge impact, such as when Paul Revere made his famous ride with the cry, "The British are coming!"

Josiah was just one person, but he made a big impact on the people in Judah. Josiah began to seek God, and this resulted in great things for Judah. Josiah wanted to purify his country of anything contrary to the worship of the living God. The spiritual reforms of King Josiah continued during his entire reign. He repaired the temple for worship. When a lost portion of Scripture was discovered, Josiah led the leaders of Judah to pledge to obey its commandments. Josiah led the people to observe the Passover celebration, something that had been abandoned for years. The end result of Josiah's reforms was that people didn't turn away from God during Josiah's lifetime.

Sure, Josiah was the king of Judah, and his influence carried a lot of weight. Still his quest to seek God started when he was a teenager, and he made a difference in the lives of many people. You may never become a person of huge influence in this world, but you do have a circle of friends whom you impact. You can make a difference in their lives right now, they can impact others, and so on. So begin to change your world and impact others for Christ—because you can make a difference.

DAILY DEVOTIONS

Day 1
2 Chronicles 34:1-5

Josiah became the king of Judah when he was only eight years old. Isn't that unbelievable? When he was about 16, he started seeking God. After Josiah's time of seeking, he made changes not only in his personal life, but also big changes in the nation of Judah. One of the positive changes he brought about was the destruction of pagan shrines and idols that had been erected after the people turned from God. Josiah even had the bones of the pagan priests burned.

Change is the result of a person—yes, even one person—who truly seeks God.

Pray this week that you'll allow God to change you to become a person of spiritual influence.

Day 2
2 Chronicles 34:14-21

During the time when the temple was being renovated, a portion of Scripture was discovered that people didn't know about. After reading the Scriptures, Josiah learned an important truth: The problems in Judah and Israel were brought on by the sinful lives of the Israelites— the people of God. Josiah discovered that God's desire was for people to obey him and follow him.

How well do the words obey and follow describe your relationship with God?

What evidence can you think of from the past days or weeks that indicates your obedience to God—or lack of it?

Day 3
Ecclesiastes 12:1-7

While this passage doesn't contain the most positive and uplifting thoughts, Solomon emphasized the importance of giving God our lives when we're young. Josiah followed God as a teenager, and God blessed him during the remainder of his reign as king.

When you're older, you'll realize that the spiritual things you did for God as a teenager made a huge impact on your life. You'll look back one day, and those memories from your youth will be priceless. Commit your life to God now. That's a decision you'll never regret. As Solomon said, "Remember God in the days of your youth."

Are you remembering God now—in the days of your youth?

Why did you respond that way?

Many good—and bad—habits are set for the rest of your life right now. Choose wisely.

Day 4
Romans 5:12-21

Let's think about that question again: Can one person really make a difference? Just one person?

Just one person—Adam—caused all of humanity to fall into sin and be separated from God. Adam was free to eat from any tree in Eden but one. He chose to rebel against God and eat of the one tree that God had forbidden. When Adam fell, all his children inherited his sin nature. We're all fallen because we're the children of Adam.

Just one person—Jesus—brought the hope of salvation to all people. Despite the fact that he was God, Jesus took on flesh and became the sacrifice for our sin. Jesus changed our eternal destiny. We were condemned to death, but in Jesus we have life.

One person can make a difference in this world—for better or for worse.

What could you do that could impact others positively—something only you could do that could make a difference in someone else's life?

Are you currently doing that? If not, why not?

Why not be a world changer?

Day 5
Psalm 33:1-11

The Bible contains many references to fearing the Lord; Josiah rediscovered what that meant. People are called to respect God and to be in awe of him.

Did you notice the awe of the psalmist in today's Scripture passage? God is right and true. God controls the movements of the earth. God controls the success or failure of the plans of the nations. The only right response to this kind of God is wonder and righteous fear.

Think about the awesome changes that would take place in your life if you were totally dependent on God.

How ready are you to live the kind of life that will bring amazing times of fellowship with God?

Would you like to see God work in wonderful ways in your life?

Would you like to have joy in your life that results from walking with God daily?

Then become totally dependent on God.

WEEK 41
PROPHET JEREMIAH: CHOSEN FOR BAD NEWS

MEMORY VERSE

"Before I formed you in the womb I knew you, before you were born I set you apart; I appointed you as a prophet to the nations." (Jeremiah 1:5)

INTRODUCTION

When I was in college, a girl from my youth group was killed in a car wreck. I hadn't seen her in five years, but the news still shocked me. The wreck happened on a weekend, and on Monday I talked with a close friend of this girl. After I told her to pass on my sympathy to the girl's family, I made a startling discovery: She'd been out of town, and no one had told her that her friend had died unexpectedly.

The prophet Jeremiah knew what it was like to be the bearer of bad news. God called Jeremiah to speak out against the sin of the people and warn them that Jerusalem would be destroyed. Needless to say, his message wasn't very popular. People plotted to kill him.

Jeremiah's prophecies were so vivid, he cried over what was about to happen. He was even nicknamed "the weeping prophet." Jeremiah always held to God's promise of protection from his enemies—and God kept his promise. After the reign of King Zedekiah, Judah was invaded by the Babylonians, and the people were taken into captivity.

People love to hear about God's love and grace, but the truth about sin, judgment, and eternal punishment isn't very popular. God may call you to risk it all and speak his truth to someone. Don't expect to be congratulated. People may respond with anger. Even so, you can be confident you'll experience the presence and protection of God.

DAILY DEVOTIONS

Day 1
Jeremiah 1:1-10

Read one more time what God told Jeremiah in verse 5. Isn't that amazing? God knew Jeremiah and set him apart for ministry even before he was born. Jeremiah's excuses were insignificant because God knew Jeremiah better than he knew himself.

If you think about it, Jeremiah isn't that different from you. God also knew you before you were born. For that matter, he knew you before Adam and Eve were created.

Have you ever wondered whether God really has a plan and purpose for your life? Wonder no more. He does. (In fact, look right now at a famous verse: Jeremiah 29:11.)

How do you view yourself? Do you ever think of yourself as insignificant? What makes you feel that way?

How does today's passage address your view of yourself?

Pray this week that God will help you be aware that he's created you for something very special.

Day 2
Jeremiah 1:11-19

When I take students on trips, I assure their parents that their teenagers will be safe and supervised. I want parents to know I'll take care of their children as if they were my very own. God called Jeremiah to speak his words, and then he gave Jeremiah the assurance that he'd watch over him and protect him. Just as I want parents to trust me with their children, you can boldly follow God's call, knowing he'll always watch over you and protect you.

Are there things in your life right now that you feel God can't handle—that he can't protect you from? If so, what are they?

Have faith that there's nothing God cannot handle—no problem is too big and no concern is too small.

Day 3
Jeremiah 8:18-9:6

Jeremiah is known as "the weeping prophet." The message God gave him concerning the destruction of Jerusalem grieved Jeremiah to the point that he wept over the sins of his people.

Does the sin you see each day grieve you?

Are you saddened by how many people have no regard for the things of God?

As Christians, it should hurt us to see the sin in our lives and in the lives of others. Maybe you need to ask God to soften your heart and make you more sensitive to the world around you.

Pray today that God will open your spiritual eyes to see sin for what it is—and to be hurt by it, repent of it, and return to him. Also pray you'll be able to share this message with others.

Day 4
Jeremiah 38:1-13

Jeremiah didn't preach feel-good messages; he preached God's message. And God's message at the time wasn't very popular. This is obvious in verses 3 and 4 of today's Scripture passage. In fact, Jeremiah's words landed him in a cistern (a deep, dug-out reservoir for holding water). Now he was trapped in mud and fighting for his life. Speaking God's truth can be dangerous, but Jeremiah was willing to take the risk.

Christians who stand on God's truth today are also likely to meet opposition. Some try to make people mad. Others don't care about the feelings of others. Neither of these positions is Christlike. But even when you share God's message in love and choose your words carefully, some people will be offended.

Are you willing to speak unpopular messages to those around you as Jeremiah did? Before you answer, remember what it cost him.

Have you ever had to suffer because you did something for God? If so, what was that like?

Pray that God would give you the strength to be a modern-day Jeremiah.

Day 5
Lamentations 3:25-39

Well-known pastor Charles Stanley once said a good father is like velvet and steel: He disciplines his children, yet loves them and shows them compassion. That's exactly how Jeremiah described God. God deals with our sin. He won't pretend nothing is wrong when we disobey him. But love is always behind his actions. Remember, when you feel God dealing with your sin, you're actually experiencing his amazing love.

How do you respond—with humbleness or rebellion—when your parents must discipline you?

It's always best for you to respond with humbleness and repentance. The same is true with God. As verse 39 says, "Why should any living man complain when punished for his sins?"

Can you think of a time when God disciplined you? What was that like? Make some notes about it as you journal.

WEEK 42
PROPHET HABAKKUK: LIVE BY FAITH

MEMORY VERSE

"See, he is puffed up; his desires are not upright—but the righteous will live by his faith." (Habakkuk 2:4)

INTRODUCTION

Do you remember Job? He was a man who suffered and wanted God to answer his questions. Habakkuk is another Old Testament character who tried to question God. Job asked why God was punishing him; Habakkuk wanted to know why God hadn't punished the nation of Judah.

Habakkuk was a prophet during the closing days of Judah's history, probably during the reign of King Jehoiakim. The prophet watched as people violated God's laws without shame. The Israelites were living as if the God who miraculously delivered their ancestors had never existed.

The first part of the book of Habakkuk records two dialogues between the prophet and God. The conversations went something like this—

> *Habakkuk: God, how can you let the sins of Judah go unpunished?*
>
> *God: I'm preparing the Babylonians as a way to judge and punish Judah.*
>
> *Habakkuk: God, why would you punish sinful Judah by using the pagan Babylonians?*
>
> *God: I will punish both Judah and the Babylonians because sin cannot go unpunished.*

The book of Habakkuk concludes with a beautiful prayer of praise sung by the prophet. Habakkuk acknowledged God as his source of strength in times of trouble. Habakkuk's questions caused him to experience God's wonder in a powerful way.

DAILY DEVOTIONS

Day 1
Habakkuk 1:1-11

Habakkuk, like Job, had some questions for God. He thought God wasn't listening to his prayers. He saw rampant sin all around him among the people who were supposed to belong to God, the people of Israel. Instead of punishing the people, God seemed to give them a pass. Habakkuk wanted to know why God didn't act.

God told Habakkuk he was aware of the actions of his people. In fact, God revealed he was raising the feared Babylonian army to teach his people a lesson. God's actions would be both timely and just.

Do you ever wonder why some people seem to get away with such awful sins?

How hard is it for you to grasp the idea of God using bad people to discipline those who sin?

Sometimes when we pray, we believe God doesn't hear us because he doesn't answer immediately. As you pray this week, remember God is always listening to your prayers. God will answer in his time and in his way—not ours—because God knows best, and we don't.

Day 2
Habakkuk 2:2-8

God spoke to a nation who believed God wasn't necessary. The people trusted in themselves and no one else. When you trust only in yourself, you end up rebelling against all authority—especially God.

You probably have a few close friends or family members you trust. Or maybe you've been betrayed, and now you believe you can trust only yourself. The road to right living begins by learning to trust in God. He'll never betray your trust.

Whom do you trust—really?

How does that trust show up in your life?

What could you do to begin to put more of your trust in God?

Reread verses 4 through 8 of today's passage. Are you like the one God describes in these verses? Or are you like the ones mentioned in verse 4—the righteous who live by faith?

Day 3
Habakkuk 3:1-7

After God answered Habakkuk's questions, Habakkuk sang a prayer that declared God's power.

God cannot tolerate sin. He could certainly crush us for our sinful lives, but he's been merciful to us by sending Jesus to die in our place. As a result, the power of God was displayed at the cross and at the tomb. He used his power to act for us instead of against us. That's something you should be thankful for each day.

Spend a few minutes thinking about how amazing God is. Then, write a prayer in this journal celebrating God's power and mercy. Thank God his mercy is just as great as his power.

Day 4
Habakkuk 3:8-19

Habakkuk lived during difficult and sinful times. God's chosen people had grown evil. They worshiped idols and had very little respect for God. Despite the awful condition of the society in which Habakkuk lived, he discovered a reason to rejoice. Why? He learned that God was in control. Whatever happens in the world, God is in control.

The world you live in can get out of control at times. There may not be many idols in your town, but we Americans can make our stuff become objects of worship. In our own way, we're as wicked as the people of Habakkuk's time. But the good news is that God is still in control.

Do you sometimes get the feeling God has forgotten you?

If so, that probably makes you feel lost and lonely. But don't fear: God hasn't forgotten you, and he still cares for you.

Pray that God will reveal to you in a special way that he's still in control of your life.

Day 5
Psalm 118:22-29

When things are going bad, it's really hard to be thankful, isn't it? But the psalmist wrote that each day is a day made by God. So whether today is sunny or cloudy, hot or cold, filled with hope or dread, a Monday or a Saturday, you can rejoice because it's a day the Lord has made. God doesn't give us all happy days because if he did, then we wouldn't appreciate them. God doesn't give us all difficult days either; he wants us to enjoy life. God gives each day as he sees best.

Do you see each day—no matter what it turns out to be—as a gift from God? Whether it's easy or not, that must be our attitude.

Thank God for what you've learned from all your days—both good ones and bad ones.

WEEK 43
PROPHET EZEKIEL: SENT TO WARN

MEMORY VERSE

"But if you do warn the wicked man to turn from his ways and he does not do so, he will die for his sin, but you will have saved yourself." (Ezekiel 33:9)

INTRODUCTION

Don't people frustrate you when their words don't match their actions? One celebrity campaigned against sport utility vehicles because they use too much gas, yet he flew in a private jet and rode in limousines. Are you ever guilty of speaking God's message but not living it? God instructed Ezekiel to live what he preached.

God chose Ezekiel to be a prophet five years after the Babylonians took Judah into captivity. He was called a watchman by God and was given the task of speaking about God's judgment and the future hope for the restoration of God's people. God described Ezekiel's audience as hard-hearted and stubborn. God also warned Ezekiel of the danger of becoming like his audience. By simply "practicing what he preached," Ezekiel could avoid that danger.

Ezekiel used unique ways to present God's message. Once God told Ezekiel to lie on his left side for 390 days to represent 390 years of Israel's sin. Then God told him to lie on his right side for 40 days to represent 40 years of Judah's sin. Ezekiel spent more than a year lying on his side.

God called Ezekiel to minister during some of the darkest days in Israel's history. His message was that God's glory had departed from his people but would one day return. Ezekiel offered the hope of restoration and future blessings from God. While Ezekiel spoke to hostile crowds, God called him to live what he preached. If he did, God promised to protect Ezekiel.

DAILY DEVOTIONS

Day 1
Ezekiel 2:1-8

God's call to Ezekiel was to speak out on God's behalf. Speaking on behalf of God Almighty must have been both a privilege and a sobering task for Ezekiel. We're called to speak for God as well.

Lots of people claim to speak for God. (If you doubt it, flip through the religious television channels sometime.) We may feel something very passionately—is that what it means to speak for God? Absolutely not. You may hear well-meaning people tell you to speak up for what you believe in. That's all well and good, as long as what you believe in isn't stupid. People can be really sincere about meaningless things.

Here's the point: You can speak for God only when you know his heart. And you'll learn God's heart only by spending time with him in his Word.

How much time are you spending listening to the heart of God as you read his Word?

If you take your job as God's spokesperson seriously, then you're his prophet in a sense.

Name some ways you're like a 21st-century prophet.

The message of God won't always be popular, but if we speak God's truth to others in a loving way, then his blessing will be on our lives.

Day 2
Ezekiel 3:4-11

We all face the danger of saying one thing but doing another. In our Christian lives, that kind of hypocrisy begins when we start speaking a message we aren't willing to live day to day. We're also hypocritical when we condemn specific sins in the lives of others—sins we're involved in ourselves. God warned Ezekiel about the danger of hypocrisy. Pray that God will help you walk the talk and talk the walk.

What are some ways you see other Christians being hypocritical?

In what ways do you struggle with hypocrisy?

Pray sincerely that you'll be convicted of any areas of your life where your words and actions aren't consistent.

Day 3
Ezekiel 33:1-9

God appointed Ezekiel as a watchman for the people of Israel. The word *watchman* means one who sees approaching danger and then warns others about it. Ezekiel was called to warn people about the danger of their sins. That wasn't a popular message back then; and because so many in our society have decided they can determine their own sense of right and wrong, it's certainly an unpopular message today. But remember that following God isn't about being popular; it's about being faithful.

Have people ever become angry with you when you spoke to them about spiritual things because they felt you were pushing your beliefs on them? How did you respond?

Don't give up. Ask God to strengthen you for the task he's called you to do: Be salt and light in the world around you.

Day 4
Psalm 75:1-10

Let's face it: When you judge other people, it's easy to let your emotions get in the way. But God is the perfect Judge. He's righteous, holy, and completely fair. He makes no mistakes. We will stand before God as our Judge one day. Will Jesus be your Defender? If he will, then you can rest in the peace of knowing you'll be found innocent of your sins.

If you've never accepted Christ as your Savior, then you don't have that assurance. Wouldn't today be a great day to make that important decision?

What will you say when you stand before God and he asks you why you should be allowed into heaven?

If you answered anything other than the fact that Jesus died for your sins, then you're trusting in the wrong things for eternal life.

Only Jesus can save you. If you're not a Christian, ask him to save you right now. Then talk to your parents, your pastor, or your youth leader about it.

Day 5
Matthew 7:1-5

If you fast-forward about 600 years from the time of Ezekiel, Jesus had something to say about judging and hypocrisy. We like to think of our own faults and sins as small and other people's as large, but Jesus said to think just the opposite: If we think of our sins as huge, then we'll have the right proportions.

Whether it was in Old Testament times or New Testament times, sin has always been a really big deal to God. He won't dwell in the presence of sin; a person has to be made right before he can stand in the presence of God.

Do you see yourself as a good person and others as sinful? If your answer is "yes," reread verses 3 through 5 of today's passage.

God's will is for you to be convicted of your own sin and to deal with it. Focusing on the sins of others doesn't help them or you.

WEEK 44
DANIEL: FIRM CONVICTIONS

MEMORY VERSE

"Now when Daniel learned that the decree had been published, he went home to his upstairs room where the windows opened toward Jerusalem. Three times a day he got down on his knees and prayed, giving thanks to his God, just as he had done before." (Daniel 6:10)

INTRODUCTION

Daniel's life was good. He was blessed with good looks. His family was well off. He was well educated. Then the Babylonians took over his country, and he was forced to live in exile. Daniel learned to make the best he could out of a bad situation.

Daniel was selected to go through special training in Babylon. He studied the language and culture of the pagan Babylonians, but Daniel never turned his back on God. Daniel kept his faith in God and his integrity, yet he still gained favor with the Babylonian rulers. That's when the trouble started.

King Darius was fond of Daniel, and he made Daniel his second in command. Some jealous peers decided to use Daniel's devotion to prayer to bring him down. The princes and administrators appealed to King Darius' vanity by having him sign a decree stating people couldn't pray to anyone except the king for 30 days. But Daniel kept on praying to God three times every day, just as he'd always done.

King Darius was trapped and forced to sentence Daniel to spend a night in a den of hungry lions. The next morning, the king raced to the lions' den and asked if God was able to deliver him. Daniel called out that he was fine because God had shut the mouths of the lions. Darius issued a new decree that everyone in the kingdom should worship Daniel's God.

Daniel went on to be a respected leader in a foreign land. He became known for his integrity and his powerful prayer life.

DAILY DEVOTIONS

Day 1
Daniel 1:8-14

Daniel and his friends were living in exile in Babylon. During a time of special training, Daniel refused to eat the food provided by the king because it violated his Jewish dietary restrictions. Daniel and his friends made a stand for their beliefs—a stand that could have cost them their lives.

You'll probably face a time when someone in authority over you wants you to compromise your convictions concerning God. It might be a coach who insists you practice instead of going to church, or a boss who insists you lie about something. When facing a demand to compromise, most people will react one of two ways: They cave and do what they're told out of fear, or they get angry and rebel against the person who asks them to compromise. Daniel did neither. He continued to show respect to those in authority over him, but he also continued to stand on his faith.

Pray this week that you'll have the courage to stand up for your Christian beliefs and the wisdom to deal with the authority over you.

Have you ever made an unpopular stand for something you knew was right? What happened?

Pray today that the story of Daniel will penetrate your mind so it's an encouragement to you the next time you face an important decision.

Day 2
Daniel 2:15-21

God gave Daniel a special ability to understand visions and dreams. Daniel used those gifts to proclaim God's power many times while he was in Babylon. Daniel and his friends also had wisdom and understanding beyond anyone else who served King Nebuchadnezzar.

God has given you many abilities and spiritual gifts as well. You may not be like Daniel in every sense, but God has given you some incredible mental and physical tools.

Are you using your gifts and abilities to honor God? How?

Pray that he'll show you how to better use your strengths and abilities for him.

Day 3
Daniel 6:1-5

Darius was moving up the ladder of political success, and he wanted to take Daniel with him. Some princes and administrators were jealous of Daniel. They looked for ways to bring him down, but they were unable to dig up any dirt on this servant of God. Daniel was a man of godly character, and he lived a life of integrity. If you're looking for a hero, pattern your life after Daniel.

If someone were looking for a way to discredit your Christian life, what would they find out about you?

Ask God to show you how to be like Daniel.

Day 4
Daniel 6:6-15

Daniel had a habit of praying each day by an open window. Then the king made a law that said you couldn't pray to anyone but him. Apparently, Daniel knew the importance of being a law-abiding citizen, but he had to choose between keeping a man-made law and praying to God. He obviously chose to keep praying.

Daniel not only continued to pray, but he also prayed with the window open. How hard would it have been to shut the window? The point is Daniel wouldn't give up his prayer life, and he wouldn't hide it. Prayer was Daniel's lifeline to God—he wouldn't compromise that at all.

How important is your prayer life to you?

Do you feel embarrassed when you're praying in public—such as at a restaurant or another place where it's appropriate to pray before a meal?

Your prayer life is a lifeline to God. Take advantage of every opportunity to pray.

Day 5
Daniel 6:16-24

During this study of Old Testament characters, we've read about many of the ways God protected his people. God miraculously protected Daniel by using an angel to shut the mouths of hungry lions. This doesn't mean that when you serve God, no harm or problems will ever come your way. There are serious problems in life—knowing God doesn't free you from those. But you can be sure that if you follow God with all your heart and with all you have, you'll be in his will—and that's the safest place in the entire world. You'll never have to face life's difficulties alone.

Are you living in a place of God's protection now—living within his will and doing what he's calling you to do? If not, what's keeping you from doing so?

Pray for God's protection, his comfort, and his peace in your life—the kind that comes from serving him.

WEEK 45
SHADRACH, MESHACH, ABEDNEGO: STANDING IN THE FURNACE

MEMORY VERSES

"If we are thrown into the blazing furnace, the God we serve is able to save us from it, and he will rescue us from your hand, O king. But even if he does not, we want you to know, O king, that we will not serve your gods or worship the image of gold you have set up." (Daniel 3:17-18)

INTRODUCTION

Shadrach, Meshach, and Abednego were Daniel's friends. In fact, all four of them were exiles from Judah living in Babylon. During King Nebuchadnezzar's three-year training period, Shadrach, Meshach, and Abednego were with Daniel. While Daniel got in trouble for his prayers, it was their failure to bow down to a gold statue that heated things up for Shadrach, Meshach, and Abednego.

King Nebuchadnezzar had a huge gold statue built. At the dedication ceremony, he declared that when people heard the music, they were to bow down to the king's statue. People of every race and language bowed to the golden idol—except Shadrach, Meshach, and Abednego. When Nebuchadnezzar heard of their refusal to bow down, he was furious and gave them one last chance to submit or face a painful death in a fiery furnace.

The confrontation between the king and these three young men was nothing short of classic. Nebuchadnezzar asked them what god could protect them in a blazing furnace, to which not just one but all three of them basically said, "The God we serve is able to save. But even if he doesn't, your majesty can be sure we'll never serve your gods or worship the gold statue you've set up."

They were willing to put their lives on the line for God. Why? Because obeying God and being faithful to him were more important to them than life itself. God did rescue Shadrach, Meshach, and Abednego from certain death in the burning furnace. And the bold stance by Shadrach, Meshach, and Abednego caused the king to issue a new declaration: "There is no other god who can rescue like this!" (Daniel 3: 29, NLT).

DAILY DEVOTIONS

Day 1
Daniel 3:8-12

King Nebuchadnezzar issued a decree. He forced people to worship a huge—90 feet tall and nine feet wide—gold statue he'd commissioned. People faced death if they didn't bow down to this giant idol.

You've probably never had anyone ask you to worship an idol. In fact, chances are no one is forcing you to put any other thing before God. Shadrach, Meshach, and Abednego were ready to die in order to remain true to God. Yet many of us fail to remain true to God when there's no opposition. When you put other things in your life before God, you do it of your own free will.

Are you guilty of choosing to worship the idols of popularity, conformity, pop culture, or a thousand other gods? God—and God alone—is deserving of our worship.

Think back over the last few days of your life. What things have you chosen to worship of your own free will?

Was God one of them? Why or why not?

Ask God to forgive you when you view other things as more important than him.

Day 2
Daniel 3:13-18

With death as a very real possibility, Shadrach, Meshach, and Abednego boldly declared they'd never serve the king's gods or worship his statue. Their faith in God was more important to them than their very lives. All they had to do was bow down to a silly idol. But they chose death over that act of disobedience. If only we could be that passionate about our faith in God.

Boldly standing up for one's faith and convictions can be costly today. Have you suffered for being a Christian?

What if it required you to suffer loss? Are you willing to pay the price?

As you pray, ask God to give you a passionate commitment to live for him without any compromise.

Day 3
Daniel 3:19-25

God protected Shadrach, Meshach, and Abednego. He didn't keep them from going into the furnace. He allowed them to walk into it, but he delivered them from a painful, fiery death—even while they were surrounded by fierce flames.

God's protection of Christians can take many forms. He may keep us far from the fires that could threaten our lives. That would be one way God could keep us safe. But he might also lead us into the flames and then protect us in the midst of them. God sometimes allows his children to suffer pain and death, but even then he protects them for eternity in heaven. God's protection is certainly not restricted to our human imagination. You probably have no idea about the many ways God is protecting you—even today.

Have you ever watched God protect you from inside a spiritual fire? If so, what was that like?

Thank God for his watchful care over you in times when you don't even realize it.

Day 4
Daniel 3:26-30

The bold faith of Shadrach, Meshach, and Abednego seared the heart of the pagan King Nebuchadnezzar. He was so amazed by the power of God to protect his people that he was prompted to say, "Praise be to…God!" (v. 28).

When you make a bold stand for Christ, even if no one says anything about it, you can be sure your actions didn't go unnoticed. And you never know: Maybe your boldness will give another Christian the courage he needs to make a stand for God.

What you do is noticed by others—Christians and non-Christians. What do you want your actions to say to believers?

What do you want to tell non-Christians through your actions?

Pray that your actions—both seen and unseen—will glorify God.

Day 5
Psalm 89:1-14

God is the originator of faithfulness. He was there for the many people in the Bible who followed him, including Shadrach, Meshach, and Abednego. God never turned his back on those who followed him.

If you're a Christian, God will always be there for you as well. The psalmist wanted to sing about the faithful love of God forever and tell all generations about it.

God has always been faithful to you. Have you always been faithful to him?

Isn't God's faithfulness worth sharing with others? Thank God today for his faithfulness in your life.

WEEK 46
DANIEL: HUMBLE, BOLD PRAY-ER

MEMORY VERSE

"O Lord, listen! O Lord, forgive! O Lord, hear and act! For your sake, O my God, do not delay, because your city and your people bear your Name." (Daniel 9:19)

INTRODUCTION

Daniel faced a den of hungry lions because of his commitment to God. The king recognized Daniel's powerful prayer life when he said, "May your God, whom you serve continually, rescue you!" God did rescue Daniel, and as his story continued to unfold, Daniel continued to pray and fast.

Daniel was grieved to learn of Jeremiah's prophecy that 70 years of desolation for Jerusalem would come to pass in Daniel's lifetime. Daniel started praying and fasting for God's people. First, he acknowledged God as a keeper of promises and confessed his sin and the sins of the Israelites. Next, Daniel recognized that the people of Israel were getting exactly what they deserved because of their disobedience and lack of trust in God. Then Daniel asked God to show mercy and turn his anger away from the sinful Israelites.

While Daniel continued to pray, a most amazing thing happened: The angel Gabriel appeared before him. The angel told Daniel his prayer had caused God to issue a message concerning one of Daniel's visions. God was also pleased with Daniel's devotion to prayer. And Gabriel even told Daniel that God loved him very much. Literally, Daniel was an object of God's delight.

Daniel was a humble man, and that meek spirit came across in his times alone with God. He was quick to repent, and he had a strong desire to seek God in all situations. Daniel was known for his character and integrity, and those qualities were strengthened through his prayer life. Daniel's prayers stirred the heart of his heavenly Father, who expressed both love and delight for his humble servant.

DAILY DEVOTIONS

Day 1
Daniel 9:1-3

Daniel was moved by the words God spoke to the prophet Jeremiah. The Scripture opened Daniel's eyes and put him on his knees in prayer. Daniel had a close encounter with God through the Scripture and an even closer encounter during his prayer time.

Take time this week to read your Bible carefully and let God's words change you. Do you spend time each day reading the Holy Scriptures and praying?

If you do, continue to do so. If not, then you're missing out on one of the greatest blessings of the Christian life.

If you aren't like Daniel (reading the Bible and praying daily), then make a commitment to God to begin doing so. Write your commitment as you journal.

Day 2
Daniel 9:4-10

Like Isaiah (see Week 37), Daniel's encounter with God made him aware of his sins. Daniel also became aware of the sins of the entire nation of Israel. There's something very important to remember here: If you're out of touch with God, then you'll be out of touch with your sinful nature. In other words, the closer you are to God, the clearer your sins will be. If you're not in touch with God, then your sins won't seem that significant.

Why did Daniel confess the sins of his people if they weren't sins he'd personally committed?

Do Christians have a duty to confess the sins of the people living in their culture and ask God for forgiveness?

Ask God to help you (1) be aware of sins, and (2) confess those sins to him. He'll forgive you.

Day 3
Daniel 9:15-19

We love to talk about how God loves people, but we sometimes hesitate to talk about his wrath. Today's passage discusses how Israel had disobeyed God and had to face the consequences of their sins. That message is harder to hear.

God does love you, but your sins will have consequences. This is how Paul put it in Galatians 6:7: "Do not be deceived: God cannot be mocked. A man reaps what he sows." Think of God's love and wrath as items balancing a scale. One is inconsistent and lacking without the other one.

Do you have a proper understanding of the mercy of God compared with the justice of God? How could you describe it (besides using the scale illustration)?

Thank God that he loves us but that his love is also tempered with discipline.

Day 4
Daniel 9:20-23

Wow! Just think about having an angel tell you God loves you and highly esteems you. Daniel's commitment to daily prayer brought about that amazing response from God.

You, too, will experience the awesome love of God when you faithfully continue to approach your heavenly Father in prayer. You may not have an angel speak to you, but you'll please the Father, and he'll smile upon you. Continue to be steadfast and faithful in prayer. Nothing in the Christian life can strengthen you, open your eyes to what God desires, or open the gates of heaven like prayer can.

How would you describe your prayer life?

What could help you have a more consistent prayer life?

Ask God to draw you to himself as you come to him in prayer.

Day 5
Psalm 25:8-14

I call it the humble circle. You cannot be humble in your own ability. Humans are too self-centered for true humility outside of God's power. Your ability to be humble comes from God's nature. As you seek God, you become more like him. Your life begins to reflect his character, and your mind begins to focus on his thoughts. As you become more like him, you become more humble. Then as you become more humble, you seek him more. As you seek him more, you become more humble. And so the circle continues.

The psalmist said the humble will be led to do what's right and will be taught the ways of the Lord. Try taking a spin in the humble circle.

Does humility scare you?

Humility often goes against our nature. The world's idea of humility seems to involve becoming a human doormat. God's idea of humility is quite different. Humility for a Christian simply means becoming more like Jesus; it means recognizing who you are—flawed and sinful—and who he is—holy and righteous.

Pray for true humility in your life.

WEEK 47
ESTHER: FOR SUCH A TIME AS THIS

MEMORY VERSE

"For if you remain silent at this time, relief and deliverance for the Jews will arise from another place, but you and your father's family will perish. And who knows but that you have come to royal position for such a time as this?" (Esther 4:14)

INTRODUCTION

Pageants are a big deal. The winners receive scholarships, cars, or even modeling contracts. Have you ever heard of a pageant to choose a queen? While in exile with the Jewish people in Persia, Esther took part in such a pageant.

King Xerxes of Persia had given a banquet that lasted six months. At its conclusion, he called for his queen to come to the party wearing her crown. When she refused his command, the king became furious and banished her from his presence. The king's attendants suggested that a search be carried out for the most beautiful women in the kingdom. These women would be presented to the king and the one who pleased him most would become the new queen of Persia.

Esther hid her Jewish background and was chosen as the new queen. Haman, the king's Prime Minister, hated Esther's uncle, a Jewish man named Mordecai. Haman conceived a plan to wipe out all the Jews. When Queen Esther was informed of Haman's plan, she determined to stop him. She risked her life by entering the presence of the king and telling him about Haman's plan. Mordecai and the rest of God's people were saved, while Haman was hanged.

Esther's part in the rescue of the Hebrew people could be seen as one great circumstance after another, but God was in control of every event in her life. Your life isn't about being in the right place at the right time. Your life—like Esther's—is a testimony to the sovereignty of God.

DAILY DEVOTIONS

Day 1
Esther 2:21-23

If you don't remember the story of how Esther became queen of Persia, scan through the first half of chapter 2. When we pick up the story in today's passage, Esther was already queen. The details of these verses may seem like a minor story within the plot, but just like any good story of intrigue, the clues are in the details. Mordecai may not have thought he was doing anything heroic when he reported the plot to kill the king. However, when Mordecai did the right thing, he set in motion a chain of events that would eventually save all the Jews in Persia.

Doing the right thing is never a small thing. In fact, it's been said there are so many small things that result in big things that there are really no small things. You may never know what big thing God will do through your small act of obedience.

Do you have a desire to always do the right thing—even when it seems like a small thing?

Can you think of a time when a small act by you or someone else ended up making a huge difference?

Pray that God will help you do the right thing in each decision you make today.

Day 2
Esther 4:4-14

The wicked Haman cooked up a plot to destroy Mordecai and all the Jews living in Persia. Of course Haman wasn't aware that the queen was Jewish. Mordecai put on clothes one would wear while grieving. His clothes caught Esther's attention, and she sent someone to find out why Mordecai was grieving. Perhaps she thought one of their relatives had died. In any case, Mordecai relayed Haman's plans and urged Esther to act.

The dilemma, of course, was that the king allowed no one to enter his presence unless they were summoned. The penalty for disobeying was death, and the death penalty could be removed only by the king. But Mordecai believed the hand of God had raised Esther to her current position. He believed Esther was queen of Persia by God's providence. Mordecai knew she'd been placed there by God to save the Jewish people from Haman's evil plot. She was literally made "for such a time as this."

God is working providentially in your life, too. Your life has both meaning and purpose. You are where you are right now because that's where God wants you. Thank him for that. And watch for what God may choose to do with you where he's placed you.

Day 3
Esther 4:15-5:3

Esther knew she must speak to the king, but to do so without an invitation could mean death. However, she was willing to take that chance to fulfill her destiny.

There are times when God wants you to do something. And when he does, believe that it's part of your divine destiny.
Do you feel God is calling you to step forward and do something specific at this point in your life?

What's keeping you from doing so? Pray that God will give you the wisdom and courage to do what he's called you to do.

Day 4
Psalm 46:1-11

There's no denying the greatness of God. Mordecai saw his great God working in the life of Esther to save her fellow Jews. David saw an even bigger picture of an almighty God who dwells among his people at all times. Today God not only dwells with us, but the Holy Spirit also lives in us.

When are you most aware of the Holy Spirit living in you?

If God is living in them, why do Christians sometimes feel far from God?

Thank God for living both in you and through you.

Day 5

1 Timothy 6:13-21

God has been the common factor in the life of each character we've studied this year—and our study of Nehemiah next week won't be any different. Every person has a small part in introducing the Lord of lords to the people of her generation—you and me included.

Now it's your turn—because you were also created for such a time as this. God can use you just as he used the people we've studied so far. What things in your life would you change to be used by God in the most effective way?

Can you honestly say you're willing and able to adjust your life to God's call?

Pray to God that you'll be usable and that he'll use you.

WEEK 48
NEHEMIAH: REBUILDING THE WALL OF JERUSALEM

MEMORY VERSE

"In fact, everyone who wants to live a godly life in Christ Jesus will be persecuted." (2 Timothy 3:12)

INTRODUCTION

Have you seen the television show during which a whole house is completely torn down and rebuilt from scratch? Viewers love to see the transformation that takes place during a rebuilding process.

Nehemiah was the original extreme makeover man, but instead of rebuilding a house, he tackled an entire city wall. A Jew living in exile in Persia, Nehemiah served as the cupbearer to King Artaxerxes I. He not only checked the wine for poisons, but he also served as a confidant to the king. When Nehemiah heard the walls of Jerusalem had been torn down, he wept, mourned, and fasted. Then he spent the next four months praying about the situation. During that time God formulated a plan in Nehemiah's mind for rebuilding the walls around Jerusalem. God also began molding Nehemiah into a spiritual leader.

Prayer played an important part in Nehemiah's life during the rebuilding of the walls. When he was given permission to return to Jerusalem, enemies of the Israelites mocked Nehemiah's plan. But his response was to pray. When those enemies threatened to attack the workers during the rebuilding process, Nehemiah prayed again about the situation. Then when rumors created discouragement among the workers, Nehemiah once more took the matter to God in prayer.

Nehemiah's passionate vision for rebuilding the walls of Jerusalem led him to discover a new level of trust in God. His spiritual leadership was stretched thin as he dealt with problem after problem, but each difficulty seemed to give him new strength. The real secret to Nehemiah's success was the thing his journey started with and centered on: Prayer.

DAILY DEVOTIONS

Day 1
Nehemiah 1:4-11

A good finish usually depends on a good start. Nehemiah started his journey of faith to rebuild the walls of Jerusalem by praying. Before he did anything else, Nehemiah spent significant time seeking God about the problem.

Isn't it amazing how often we embark on some task without first praying if we should even undertake it? Prayer is often a last resort, not the first step. Make sure prayer is a part of the beginning of anything you plan to do. There's no job so big or so small that it shouldn't be prayed about.

Why is prayer so important in making decisions about whether or not to do something?

Do you bathe your decisions in prayer? Why or why not?

As odd as it sounds, pray that you'll be a pray-er (a praying person).

Day 2
Nehemiah 4:1-5

Nehemiah not only started his task with prayer, but he also prayed over each step along the way. In other words, he didn't just use prayer at the beginning of the project and then do things his own way. He went to God in prayer before the task began, and then he prayed often as the work continued. When the opposition mocked him, Nehemiah turned the matter over to God in prayer.

Are you sometimes quick to abandon a project when other people make fun of you? Why?

Start with prayer and—just as importantly—continue in prayer. Pray every step of the way.

Day 3
Nehemiah 4:10-23

The tide of public opinion can turn very quickly. Nehemiah's workers were becoming discouraged, so he prayed. God gave him the right words of encouragement to speak to the people.

Have you ever realized how much impact your words can have on others? Your words really do have the power to hurt or to heal.

How have your words been used recently? Would you be classified as a hurter or a healer?

Ask God to help you be an encourager, not a discourager.

Day 4
Nehemiah 5:14-19

Nehemiah led by example. Even though he was the governor of Jerusalem, he didn't ask for or accept any special favors. He wanted to be treated just like everyone else.

A godly leader is a servant. She has the heart of a servant, acts like a servant, and speaks like a servant. If you want to be a great leader, you must first learn to be a great servant.

What are the characteristics of a leader who wants to be the boss?

What are the characteristics of a servant-leader?

Which set of characteristics is godlier?

Ask God to give you the wisdom to know how to be a servant when you're placed in a role of authority.

Day 5
Proverbs 29:18-27

Solomon said that where there's no one to speak the truth of the Bible—God's vision for his people—people will perish. Godly vision comes from people who are in touch with God through prayer and his Word. That's what made Nehemiah a great man of vision: It was God's vision, not his.

What a great place to end our study of the people of the Old Testament! You've seen God touch many people—and you've studied how he used those people to touch others. But the point of it all is that God desires to use you. If you want a God-centered vision for your life both now and in the future, spend consistent time alone with your heavenly Father in prayer and in his Word. Listen to what God is saying to you and then obey him. You may be one of the mighty leaders he's calling to bring his Word to our generation.

What's the difference between having a vision for something and having God's vision for it?

Which makes more sense? Which is more difficult?

Worship God today...the God of Abraham, Isaac, and Jacob...the God who rescued his people from the Philistines, the Assyrians, and the Persians...the God who spoke through his prophets and guided his kings. Worship the God of all history.

Then ask God to give you great vision. Ask God to help you draw near to him so you can know his heart. Ask him to use you in whatever way he chooses for this time and with this generation.

A FINAL WORD

We pray this book has impacted your life and challenged the way you view God. Although we've looked at the people of the Old Testament, the Old Testament's message isn't just about the people. It's about God. He's the one who impacted the characters. And he still impacts lives today.

The same God who created the world with a word is reaching out to you. God has a plan for your life. God's called you into a relationship with him.

Hebrews 11:1-2 says, "Now faith is being sure of what we hope for and certain of what we do not see. This is what the ancients were commended for." The Old Testament characters were "sure" and "certain" of things they didn't completely understand, and God commended them for it.

God also calls us to do things we don't perfectly understand. Our walk with God is a faith walk. Though we haven't actually seen God with our eyes, we believe God exists. We haven't heard God's voice with our ears, but we know God speaks to us. We haven't touched God with our hands, but we've been in God's presence.

God never changes. God moved in the lives of these Old Testament people, and God will do the same for you. Know God's character. Place your faith in God. After all, the journey's just begun.